Journey of Faith

a Junior High Bible Study Collection

Concordia Publishing House

Copyright © 2007 Concordia Publishing House
3558 S. Jefferson Ave., St. Louis, MO 63118-3968
1-800-325-3040 • www.cph.org

All rights reserved. Unless specifically noted, no part of this publication may be reproduced, stored in a retrieval system, or transmitted, in any form or by any means, electronic, mechanical, photocopying, recording, or otherwise, without the prior written permission of Concordia Publishing House.

The purchaser of this publication is allowed to reproduce the marked portions contained herein for classroom use. These resources may not be transferred or copied to another user.

Portions originally published by Concordia Publishing House, copyright © 1999, 2000, 2001, 2002, 2003, 2004.

Written by Nicole Dreyer, Jim Elsner, Gretchen Gebhardt, Steven Graebner, Barrie Henke, Kirk Hille, Brian King, James Klawiter, Reynold Kremer, Glen Lucas, Kurt Mews, William Moorhead, Beth Murphy, Max Murphy, Rebecca Peters, Jay Reed, Mark Rhoads, Greg Rommel, Nikki Rochester, Christine Ross, Matthew Schaefer, Karin Semler, Roger Sonnenberg, Julie Steigemeyer, Susan Voss, Malinda Walz, Cynthia Werner, and Karen Westbrooks.

Edited by Mark S. Sengele

Scripture quotations are taken from the HOLY BIBLE, NEW INTERNATIONAL VERSION®. NIV®. Copyright © 1973, 1978, 1984 by International Bible Society. Used by permission of Zondervan Publishing House. All rights reserved.

Your comments and suggestions concerning the material are appreciated. Please write to the Editor of Youth Materials, Concordia Publishing House, 3558 S. Jefferson Avenue, St. Louis, MO 63118-3968.

This publication may be available in braille, in large print, or on cassette tape for the visually impaired. Please allow 8 to 12 weeks for delivery. Write to Lutheran Blind Mission, 7550 Watson Rd., St. Louis, MO 63119-4409; call toll-free 1-888-215-2455; or visit the Web site: www.blindmission.org.

Manufactured in the United States of America

1 2 3 4 5 6 7 8 9 10   16 15 14 13 12 11 10 09 08 07

Table of Contents

Lesson	Title	Bible Story	Page
1	**Against All Odds**	Prophecy of the Savior	6
2	**God's Logo**	The Word Becomes Flesh	8
3	**The Plan**	Birth of John Foretold	10
4	**Jumping for Joy**	Birth of Jesus Foretold	12
5	**Bundle of Joy**	Birth of John the Baptizer	14
6	**God, Understated**	Birth of Jesus	16
7	**From Grunge to Glory**	Announcement to the Shepherds	18
8	**Godly Role Models**	Jesus' Presentation at the Temple	20
9	**The Greatest Gift**	Visit of the Wise Men	22
10	**The Holy Refugee Family**	Flight into Egypt	24
11	**Family Matters**	Boy Jesus in the Temple	26
12	**Preparing God's Way**	John the Baptizer	28
13	**Be Radical**	John and the Baptism of Jesus	30
14	**Trouncing Temptation**	Temptation of Jesus	32
15	**Calling All Sinners**	Jesus Calls Matthew	34
16	**Jesus Calls Disciples**	Jesus Calls Philip and Nathanael	36
17	**Demons Defeated**	Jesus Heals a Demon-Possessed Man	38
18	**A Battle of Wills**	Jesus Cleanses a Leper	40
19	**The Real Deal**	Jesus Heals a Paralytic	42
20	**In Moments of Need**	Jesus Heals a Woman	44
21	**Why Trust?**	Jesus Heals Many	46
22	**Why Did This Happen?**	Jesus Heals a Man Born Blind	48
23	**Even the Wind and the Waves**	Jesus Calms a Storm	50
24	**Cleaning House**	Jesus Clears the Temple	52
25	**Measuring Up**	Pharisees Criticize the Disciples	54
26	**Newborn**	Jesus and Nicodemus	56
27	**Living Water**	Jesus and the Woman at the Well	58

Lesson	Title	Bible Story	Page
28	**Father Loves Best**	Parable of the Prodigal Son	60
29	**Who's My Neighbor?**	Parable of the Good Samaritan	62
30	**Lord, If You Had Been There**	Jesus Raises Lazarus from the Dead	64
31	**Who Is the Greatest?**	The Greatest in the Kingdom of Heaven	66
32	**Bless You!**	Jesus Blesses the Children	68
33	**Money Matters**	Jesus Is Anointed	70
34	**Servant Leadership**	Jesus Washes the Disciples' Feet	72
35	**Three Words from the Cross**	Jesus and the Thief on the Cross	74
36	**New View of an Old Story**	Jesus' Crucifixion and Resurrection	76
37	**Miraculous Fishing and Love**	Jesus Appears to His Disciples	78
38	**Ignited by God's Word**	On the Road to Emmaus	80
39	**I'm Supposed to Do What?**	The Great Commission	82
40	**What Did You Say?**	God Sends the Holy Spirit	84
41	**Rejoicing in God's Power**	Peter and John Heal	86
42	**To-Do List**	Stephen	88
43	**Searching for Wholeness**	Philip and the Ethiopian	90
44	**It's a God Thing**	The Conversion of Saul	92
45	**Being Bold**	Paul's First Missionary Journey	94
46	**Energized Encouragers!**	Barnabas	96
47	**God's Gift**	The Early Church	98
48	**God, a Guy Named Timothy, and Me**	Timothy	100
49	**This Way or That Way?**	Lydia	102
50	**Fearless Faith**	Paul and Silas in Prison	104
51	**Is Ignorance Bliss?**	Paul and Silas	106
52	**God *Is* in Control**	Paul's Shipwreck	108

Introduction

Junior high students live in a confusing and increasingly complicated world. Their lives are often conflicted and torn as a result of sin. Sometimes it is sin from within, expressing itself in actions and attitudes that run counter to God's Law. Sometimes it is sin from other sources—the actions and attitudes of others—that disrupts their lives. They need God's help to live in the joy and fullness that Christ desires.

Since it is the Gospel that brings spiritual life in Christ to people, it is our goal in these Bible studies for junior high students to connect the Gospel to their life situations. These studies were prepared with four goals in mind. The lessons reflect these goals in the following ways:

1. Each lesson presents the Gospel in ways that will help young people grow in their relationship with Christ.

2. Each lesson is simple and direct—one page of instructions and helps for the Bible study leader and one reproducible page for the students to follow.

3. Each study is practical and easy to prepare. Interaction, variety, and active learning are stressed without requiring excessive preparation by the Bible study leader.

4. Each study deals with the Bible text and seeks to help young people apply the lesson to their lives as they seek to live in Christ.

This book contains fifty-two studies. They can be selected according to the needs of the students and leader and taught in any order.

HELPS FOR PREPARATION AND TEACHING

For ease of use, the leader page and student page for each study are printed side by side in this book, the leader's material on the left and the corresponding student page on the right. The appropriate student page should be copied in a quantity sufficient for the class and distributed at the time indicated in the leader's notes.

It is assumed that the Bible class leader will have the usual basic classroom equipment and supplies available—pencils or pens for each student, blank paper (and occasionally tape or marking pens), and a chalkboard or its equivalent (white board, overhead transparency projector, or newsprint pad and easel) with corresponding chalk or markers. Encourage the students to bring their own Bibles so that they can mark useful passages and make personal notes to guide their Bible study between classes. Do provide additional Bibles, however, for visitors or students who do not bring one.

The studies are outlined completely in the leader's notes, including a suggested amount of time for each section of the study. The suggested times will total fifty to fifty-five minutes, the maximum amount most Sunday morning Bible classes have available. Each session begins with an opening activity that may or may not be indicated on the student page. Teachers who regularly begin with prayer should include it before the opening activity. Most other parts of the study, except the closing prayer, are on both the leader page and student page.

An average class size of ten students is assumed. To facilitate discussion, especially when your class is larger than average, it is recommended that you conduct much of the discussion in smaller breakout groups—pairs, triads, or groups of five or six. Instructions to that effect are often included in the guide. If your class is small, you are blessed to already have a "breakout group" and can ignore these suggestions. Leaders who prefer to do all discussion with the class as a whole are also free to ignore breakout-group suggestions.

Most of the studies include one or two "Lesson Extenders" suggestions. Use these when the study progresses more quickly than expected, when your normal session exceeds fifty to fifty-five minutes, or when a suggested activity doesn't work with your group. They can also be used as "during the week" activities.

Of course, the leader is encouraged to review the study thoroughly, well in advance of its presentation. That way the materials can be tailored to your individual students' needs and preferences as well as your own. A prepared and confident teacher normally has better classroom control, which results in a more positive experience for both students and leader.

1. Against All Odds

Isaiah 7:14
Lesson Focus
God strengthens our faith with His promises.

WHERE DO WE BEGIN?
(10 minutes)

You may choose to provide some background information about Old Testament prophecy: God used ordinary people to convey His very words concerning past, present, and future events. God's words pertaining to future events at the time they were given are divine promises, or prophecies. Many of these prophecies pertain to the Messiah, Jesus Christ.

There are sixty major prophecies in the Old Testament concerning the Messiah. Mathe-maticians have figured out that the probability of just eight of these prophecies coming true in one person is 1 in 100,000,000,000,000,000 (10 to the seventeenth power). This would be like having a blindfolded person looking for one marked coin in a sea of coins two feet deep that covers the entire state of Texas. What does the fact that all sixty major prophecies came true in Christ mean to you? (Answers will vary; God has an excellent track record.) What assurance does this information give you? (He has always, and will always, keep His promises.)

GETTING INTO IT
(20 minutes)

Read the prophecy recorded in Isaiah 7:14. King Ahaz, the man to whom the prophecy of the virgin birth was originally given, needed some assurance. A troubled man, he shut the doors of the temple and worshiped idols. Beginning with Ahaz's example, what might be some causes for a person's lack of faith? (In Ahaz's case, not being in true worship/fellowship with other believers and not reading Scripture; other answers may be given under different circumstances.) Ahaz was given the opportunity to ask God for a sign, or promise, that this enemy would be defeated, but he foolishly declined. However, God gave him the sign of Immanuel anyway. What does this say about God? (God's grace does not depend on our strength of faith.) This sign was fulfilled in both Ahaz's situation—his enemies were annihilated—and, more important, in the coming of the Messiah. Read Matthew 1:18–25. What does this say about the measure of God's grace? (God gives it abundantly, beyond our limited scope of expectations.)

A CLOSER LOOK
(15 minutes)

Like Ahaz, some people turn away from God and His Word when doubts throw shadows on their faith. Why is this ironic? (They cut themselves off from the source of good things.) What Scripture verses provide you with assurance in tough times? Share them with a partner or the group. Close with prayer: "Father, Your Word is truth. You know all things that have been and are yet to come. You see our sin. Forgive us for not always looking to You, and lead us to follow Your ways. Thank You for always keeping Your Word. In Jesus' name. Amen."

LESSON EXTENDER

✝ Look up the following messianic prophecies and list how each one was fulfilled in Christ: Daniel 9:25 (born during a decree); Isaiah 7:14 (born of a virgin); Micah 5:2 (born in the town of Bethlehem); Hosea 11:1 (flight to Egypt); Isaiah 53:3 (rejected and despised); Zechariah 9:9 (rode a colt/Palm Sunday); Psalm 41:9 (betrayed); Isaiah 53:7 (silent before Pilate); Isaiah 53:5 (sacrificed); Zechariah 12:10 (pierced); Psalm 22:7 (mocked); Psalm 16:10; 49:15 (resurrection); Psalm 68:18 (ascended to heaven).

Against All Odds

WHERE DO WE BEGIN?

There are sixty major prophecies in the Old Testament about the Messiah. Mathematicians have figured the probability of just eight of these prophecies coming true in one person as 1 in 100,000,000,000,000,000 (10 to the seventeenth power). This would be like having a blindfolded person looking for one marked coin in a sea of coins two feet deep that covers the entire state of Texas.

What does the fact that all sixty major prophecies came true in Christ mean to you?

....
....
....

What assurance does this information give you?

....
....

GETTING INTO IT

Read **Isaiah 7:14**.

Beginning with Ahaz's example, what might be some causes for a person's lack of faith?

....
....

Despite Ahaz's lack of trust and faith, God gave him the sign of Immanuel anyway. What does this say about God?

....
....

God allowed Ahaz to overcome his enemies. What does this say about the measure of God's grace?

....
....

A CLOSER LOOK

Like Ahaz, some people turn away from God and His Word when doubts throw shadows on their faith. Why is this ironic?

....
....
....

What Scripture verses provide you with assurance in tough times?

....
....
....

Journey of Faith © 2007 Concordia Publishing House. Reproduced by permission.

STUDENT PAGE 1

2. GOD'S LOGO

John 1:1–18

Lesson Focus

Through this study, students will realize that, in Christ, all spiritual and physical needs are satisfied, putting the appeals of earthly advertising into proper perspective.

LOGOS (10 minutes)

Distribute copies of the student page and discuss the first question, or display several common trademarks, especially those that are just symbols, and see if your students can identify them. (For a challenge, record several "audio logos" such as those used by Intel, the computer chip manufacturer, or AT&T.) After the logos have been identified, ask the second student page question: "Why do companies invest in strong logos?" (To connect consumers with certain products in the hope that they will purchase these familiar "name brands.") Do your students think this works? Can they easily identify the logos of products they regularly buy and use? (Probably quite well.)

Point out that God also is in "business." He has a "trademark" and "advertises." Direct the students to the next section of the student page.

WHAT GOD SAYS (20 minutes)

Have a volunteer read aloud John 1:1–18. Then ask what God's logo might be. Share with the students, "The word *logo*, that we use for business trademarks, is taken from the Greek word *logos* (LAH-gahs), meaning 'word.' In John 1:1, the Bible calls Jesus the *Logos*—the Word made flesh." Discuss the student page questions, checking the students' responses with this information:

1. Point out that Christ is God's visible "logo." More than any earthly corporation's logo, Jesus truly communicates God's product.

2. God's product is grace (undeserved kindness). His product is given away—at no cost to us, but at the great cost of Jesus' suffering and death.

3. Read through the passage again, challenging the students to pinpoint gifts of God's grace. They include verse 3: creation; verse 4: new life; verse 9: spiritual knowledge which eventually leads to righteousness (see also Romans 3:21–24); verse 10: creation; verse 12: membership in God's family; verse 14: God living among us (see also Matthew 1:23—"*Immanuel*"); verse 16: blessings; verse 17: grace and truth; verse 18: seeing God in the flesh (Christ).

PUTTING THE WORD INTO USE (15 minutes)

Allow the students to respond to the student page questions. Then point out the world's reaction to God's grace and *logos*—verse 5: Jesus is not understood; verse 10: He is not recognized (as true God); verse 11: He is not accepted (as the Messiah) by those who should know better. Point out that, by the Spirit's power, Christians respond to God's grace with praise and worship—and with acts of service. Invite the students to suggest ways they can be more active in these fruits of faith.

CLOSING (5 minutes)

Have each class member draw a logo or write a product name on a piece of paper and identify a spiritual blessing suggested by that logo (Nike's "swoosh": the shoes of the Gospel of Peace [Ephesians 6:15]; Allstate's "good hands": the nail-marked hands of Christ [John 20:27]). Exchange logos and have each student pray that God grant that spiritual blessing to the participants in this study.

LESSON EXTENDER

✝ Help the students describe how people reject God's logo and His grace with specific terms and examples. (Evolution, self-justification, self-promotion, Christ-less worship, etc.)

✝ In a twenty-four hour span, how do you think God's product—grace—will be evident in your life? (Keep track for one day this week!)

8

GOD'S LOGO

LOGOS
Most companies have logos, designs that appear in their ads and on their products to create instant identification. What are some common logos you know?

Some companies pay thousands of dollars for the creation of the logos. Why do companies invest in strong logos?

WHAT GOD SAYS
Read **John 1:1–18**. Then consider the following questions.

1. How is Jesus Christ a perfect logo?

2. What "product" does God handle? How much does it cost?

3. Pinpoint the key "product information" found in these verses:

Verse 3:

Verse 4:

Verse 9:

Verse 10:

Verse 12:

Verse 14:

Verse 16:

Verse 17:

Verse 18:

PUTTING THE WORD INTO USE
What was the world's reaction to God's product? (See **John 1:5**, **10**, and **11**.)

How can you as a Christian respond to God's gift of grace?

STUDENT PAGE 2

Journey of Faith © 2007 Concordia Publishing House. Reproduced by permission.

3. THE PLAN

Luke 1:5–25

Lesson Focus

God's plan of salvation defies our human logic, yet through His plan all of humankind is offered salvation through the death and resurrection of Christ.

HOW I'D SAVE THE WORLD (10 minutes)

Begin the lesson by telling your class, "I want each one of you to take a couple of minutes to come up with a plan to save the world." Give your students time to think, then ask each student to share his or her plan. Encourage the class to discuss the various ideas presented and how effective their plan would be at actually saving the world. After a few minutes, say something like, "What if I said, 'I'll just kill one person, and the world will be saved'? Do you think your non-Christian friends would think that was crazy? Sometimes we forget what a scandal God's plan to save the world is, but today's Bible lesson reminds us that, as wild as it is, it is based on historical facts that have real meaning for our lives today."

JUST THE FACTS (15 minutes)

Distribute student pages and ask students to look up Luke 1:5–25. Direct students to follow the directions in this section on the student page. When students have finished filling in their sheets, ask, "Which of these facts do you think are most important and why? Why is this particular story important in God's plan of salvation? Why do you think this story is included here? Why is it important that the Bible contains so many historical dates, places, and facts?"

Explain that this story of the birth of John the Baptist is God's way of continuing to unfold His plan of salvation. Luke records this story so we can understand who John was and what he was sent to do. It is an important story because it fulfills prophecy (Matthew 17:9–13) and shows how God is involved in working His plan in and through the daily lives of His people. Knowing the facts of Scripture reminds us that God forgives sin and gives eternal life through the historical, factual death and resurrection of Jesus. God's gift of salvation is not a faint dream, but a real hope anchored in the real life and work of His Son on our behalf.

A PLAN TO SHARE THE FACTS (15 minutes)

Direct students' attention to this section of the student page. Invite them to list the name of a friend who is not a Christian. Then ask students to think about that person and write down any "openings" they can think of. Openings are hurts, fears, or challenges in a friend's life that might make him or her open to the Gospel. For instance, someone may be struggling with loneliness or depression, parents' divorce, or even something like a big test coming up. Next, ask students to think of Jesus Christ's life and words. What acts of Jesus or Bible verses come to mind that might apply to their friend's situation? Encourage students to work together in sharing friends' situations and brainstorming possible Gospel "facts" that they might share. Ask them to record these facts on the student page.

CLOSING (5 minutes)

Wrap up your time by asking class members to pray for the friends they listed on their paper. Close by reciting the Apostles' Creed together.

THE PLAN

JUST THE FACTS

Sometimes God's plan for saving the world is so familiar to us that we take the facts for granted. Take a few minutes to review **Luke 1:5–25**, and then fill in the blanks.

The main two people:
(verses 5–7) .... and ....

The place:
(verses 8–9) ....

The messenger:
(verses 11, 19) ....

The Plan

Name:
(verse 13) ....

Description:
(verses 14–15) ....

His purpose:
(verses 16–17) ....
....

The proof:
(verses 19–20) ....

The witnesses:
(verses 21–22) ....
....

The testimony:
(verses 23–25) ....
....
....
....

A PLAN TO SHARE THE FACTS

Friend's name ....

Openings (hurts, fears, challenges):
....

Five facts about Jesus that my friend needs to hear:

1. ....

2. ....

3. ....

4. ....

5. ....
....

STUDENT PAGE 3

Journey of Faith © 2007 Concordia Publishing House. Reproduced by permission.

4. JUMPING FOR JOY

Luke 1:26–55; Philippians 4:4–9

Lesson Focus

Jesus came to earth to be our Savior. He gives us reason to rejoice and opportunities to express our joy.

JUMP IN! (5 minutes)

Distribute copies of the student page. Allow students time to imagine the best news they could receive, what they would do, and how they would feel.

A MESSAGE FOR MARY (15 minutes)

Read **Luke 1:26–45** together, and discuss the facts of the story. The virgin birth of Jesus occurred because He was conceived by the Holy Spirit, making Him both God and man. Mary's strong faith is seen in her response and her willingness to be part of this miracle. Inspired by the Holy Spirit, Elizabeth praises Mary's faith. We honor Mary as an example of faith and service, but not as one who can answer prayers or do miracles. Mary rejoiced that her Savior from sin was to be born. We rejoice in the same Good News.

REASONS TO REJOICE (10 minutes)

Read together Luke 1:46–55. As you discuss why the selected words bring us joy, emphasize the greatness of God and His love for us as seen in His plan to save us from our sins.

JUMPING TO CONCLUSIONS (15 minutes)

The statements are intentionally ambiguous. Be careful to study them in light of Philippians 4:4–9 and not according to human wisdom.

1. Our sinful nature causes us to worry. God's Spirit leads us to faith through the Word and strengthens us to live as God's children. We rejoice in the Lord and praise Him for His goodness, trusting in Him for the future.

2. Christians mourn sin and its effects in the world as Jesus did at Lazarus's tomb, but at the same time we recognize our victory over these evils because of Christ's resurrection. When we are anxious, we pray and trust God to act for our good.

3. These verses do not merely advocate positive thinking. God wants us to center our thoughts on Him and on what He has done and is doing for us.

4. Though earthly pleasures may make us happy, this is only temporary. Our joy will only be complete once we reach our heavenly home. Without Christ there is no forgiveness, no love, no salvation, and, thus, no reason to rejoice.

I'VE GOT THE JOY! (10 minutes)

Allow students time to share from their own experiences, and be ready with examples of your own. Encourage students to express their joy through singing praises, prayers, or acts of service. You may wish to plan a time to sing Christmas carols in a hospital, nursing home, or to shut-ins. Invite students to choose a closing hymn to sing together that brings joy to their hearts.

LESSON EXTENDER

✝ Recall the attributes of God as listed in Luther's Small Catechism (question 93), and note how they are directly included or implied in Mary's hymn of praise.

✝ Challenge students to list items they would include in their own hymn of praise. Then invite each student to read a phrase or two to which the class responds in litany form, "My spirit rejoices in God my Savior" (Luke 1:47).

JUMPING FOR JOY

JUMP IN!
Can you imagine getting a message that caused you to jump for joy? Whom might it be from? What would it say?

....

....

....

A MESSAGE FOR MARY
Read **Luke 1:26–45**.

What did the angel tell Mary?

....

How does Mary's response show her faith?

....

How do Elizabeth and John the Baptist respond to the news?

....

Where is the hope for us in this message?

....

....

REASONS TO REJOICE
Read Mary's song in **Luke 1:46–55**. Explain why the following words or phrases are reasons to rejoice.

Savior **(verse 47)**

....

He has been mindful **(verse 48)**

....

The Mighty One **(verse 49)**

....

Mercy **(verse 50)**

....

Mighty deeds **(verse 51)**

....

Good things **(verse 53)**

....

Forever **(verse 55)**

....

JUMPING TO CONCLUSIONS
Read **Philippians 4:4–9** and choose one of the following statements to defend or deny.

1. You cannot worry while you are rejoicing.

....

2. Christians should never be sad. (See also **John 11:35**.)

....

3. The key to being happy is to think happy thoughts. (For help see **Romans 12:2** and **Hebrews 12:2–3**.)

....

4. Without Christ there is no reason to rejoice.

....

I'VE GOT THE JOY!
What reasons do you have for rejoicing?

....

How can you express this joy?

....

Journey of Faith © 2007 Concordia Publishing House. Reproduced by permission.

5. Bundle of Joy

Luke 1:57–80

Lesson Focus

Teens can be sure that, just as John brought great joy to his parents, God gave each of us a new birth at our Baptism, which gives joy to us, our parents, and even the angels in heaven.

Joy, Joy, Joy, Joy
(10 minutes)

Distribute copies of the student page. Have all the students line up in the middle of the room. Go through each item and ask students to identify which of the two choices brings more joy. If it is the first choice, go to the left side of the room. If it is the second choice, go to the right side of the room. After you have read all the statements, have the students sit down again. If space does not allow for students to move about, you may choose to have students discuss their choices in breakout groups.

Joy at Christmas
(20 minutes)

Have the students make their Christmas wish list. Let them put anything on it that they sincerely want for a present. Ask them the questions that follow. Have students work in breakout groups to share their lists and respond to the questions. Say to the students, "John's parents had waited and prayed for a child for many years. They thought they would never have one, but God gave them a baby in their old age. Do you think they loved and appreciated that baby? The birth of John brought much joy to their family and friends. Let's look at the story a little closer."

Have the students read Luke 1:57–67 and answer the questions. Discuss their answers as a whole group.

Everyone rejoiced because of the miracle. Elizabeth was past childbearing age, so this child was a gift from God. It was a custom to name a son after his father. A son could carry on his father's name after his aging father had passed away, which often helped with the family business. John was not even the name of any relative. Without understanding God's plan, the people did not know why his parents would come up with such a name. John was truly a gift or a miracle from God. John was also the gift from God that would point the way to the ultimate gift, Jesus Christ, and the salvation of the world. John's parents realized he was something special from God. They recognized that he had a purpose to his life. Zechariah sang the song that follows in verses 68–79. He had much joy, not only because he now had a son, but because he recognized God's plan of salvation that would come through the Messiah.

Sing for Joy
(15 minutes)

As you ask the students the questions, point out that every worship service is our opportunity to sing for joy to God. We do it in many different places in the service. But more important, as you read the Scripture verses, be sure to help students understand that Baptism is a rebirth in the Spirit of God in which He gives us a new identity as His children. He gives us this new identity as He washes away our sins and makes us perfectly clean again. He doesn't see us as the sinners we are, but as His redeemed sons and daughters who bring Him much joy.

Closing (15 minutes)

Close the session with prayer, making note of any special prayer requests that students may have.

BUNDLE OF JOY

JOY, JOY, JOY, JOY
What brings you the most joy?

Making an A on a test or spending an afternoon with your friends?

Winning a ball game or receiving a $20 gift?

The end of the school year or the beginning of the school year?

Christmas presents or Christmas vacation?

Staying up late or sleeping in?

Reading a great book or watching a good movie?

Going to a party with your friends or going on a date with someone special?

JOY AT CHRISTMAS
What do you want for Christmas?

How will you feel if you don't get it? How will you feel if you do get it? Why?

Have you ever had to wait a long time for something? What was your attitude toward it and your use of it after you got it?

Read **Luke 1:57–67**.
Why did everyone rejoice when Elizabeth had her baby?

Why did the people want to name him after his father?

Why were they surprised when both Elizabeth and Zechariah said to name him John?

John means "gift from God." Why was this name so fitting? What did it have to do with the birth of Jesus?

What did the people realize in **verse 66**?

What was Zechariah's reaction to the birth of John?

SING FOR JOY
What makes you feel like singing?

In what part of the worship service do you personally express to God the joy you feel? Songs, prayers, sermon, offering, Communion, confession, or other times?

Read **2 Corinthians 5:17**. Why does God give you a new identity in your Baptism?

What does this say about how God feels about you? Read **Galatians 3:26–27**.

Journey of Faith © 2007 Concordia Publishing House. Reproduced by permission.

6. GOD, UNDERSTATED

Luke 1:39–56; 2:1–20

Lesson Focus

God often chooses to do His work using normal people in quiet, unnoticed ways. Today's lesson looks at how God used such ordinary people to bring the Savior down to earth.

GETTING STARTED (10 minutes)

Have the students discuss the student page scenario—a Hollywood rewrite of God's original story of the birth of Jesus. Discuss the world's preoccupation with entertainment value, particularly that which appeals to our sinful human nature.

GOD AT WORK (20 minutes)

Have volunteers read **Luke 1:39–45**. Mary's visit to her cousin Elizabeth and the reaction of Elizabeth's unborn child are all within the normal activities of people. But at the same time, God used these normal events to further the plan of salvation.

Read **Luke 1:46–55**. This song of Mary (called the Magnificat) was one of the early songs of the Christian Church. Have the students pick out phrases that would be meaningful to a persecuted, struggling Church. Point out that we experience similar situations and also need to hear God's message.

Read **Luke 2:1–20**. Many of your students could probably recite from memory this most famous of stories. Have them (with your help) point out how normal most of these events were (young couple expecting, crowded city, poor accommodations, birth, strange visitors). The one spectacular event was the message of the angels to the shepherds.

Have students share their observations. Focus the discussion on why God chose to bring His Son into the world in this way, rather than in ways Hollywood might invent. God came to humankind in a non-threatening manner, in the form of a helpless infant.

The message of the angels was that, through Christ, the warfare between God and humans was over. God had unilaterally, unconditionally, and at great cost ended it.

GOD AT WORK IN YOU (15 minutes)

Challenge the students to imagine that they are any of the people in the Christmas story (including Jesus). Have them tell what effect the coming of Christ in the flesh would have on them.

Encourage the students to consider sharing their own faith story. Help them see the events (Baptism, Bible study, Holy Communion, and others) and people (parents, sponsors, teachers, and friends) through which God has worked the miracle of Christ's coming in them.

CLOSING (5 minutes)

Have the students write a one-line statement of praise similar to that of the angels' song, "Glory to God in the highest, and on earth peace to men on whom His favor rests" (Luke 2:14).

LESSON EXTENDER

✝ Have the students work together to write a modern Magnificat to tell about what God has done in their lives.

16

GOD, UNDERSTATED

GETTING STARTED
Suppose Matthew or Luke were to submit his account of the birth of Jesus to Hollywood for a made-for-television movie.

What might the producers want to rewrite? Why?

GOD AT WORK
Read **Luke 1:39–45**. How did God use normal activities of normal people to accomplish His work?

Read **Luke 1:46–55**. Pick out examples of God's acts that the members of the Early Christian Church would eagerly remember.

Read **Luke 2:1–20**. In this well-known story, which events might have the only "Hollywood-like" appeal?

Why do you think God chose the shepherds to witness the message of the angels?

Why do you think God chose to bring His Son into the world in this way?

GOD AT WORK IN YOU
How did God work His plan of salvation in you?

What events resulted in your faith?

What people have shared His story with you?

STUDENT PAGE 6

Journey of Faith © 2007 Concordia Publishing House. Reproduced by permission.

7. FROM GRUNGE to GLORY

Luke 2:1–20;
1 Corinthians
1:27–31

Lesson Focus

The students will discover God's grace in calling lowly shepherds to see and spread His salvation and will be empowered to follow the shepherds' example, glorifying God in their own work.

THE WORST WORK
(15 minutes)

Distribute copies of the student page and instruct students to complete part 1, describing the worst work they ever had. *Don't let them show their answer to anyone.*

Then ask three volunteers to act out their "worst jobs" for the class to guess. Have the students explain what was so bad about their particular job and describe anything good about it.

OUT STANDING IN THEIR FIELD (10 minutes)

Assign two students the parts of a narrator and an angel and have them read Luke 2:8–20, with the rest of the class reading the part of the shepherds. Have the students mark the poll on the student page and invite a show of hands to find out what part of shepherding the students would have hated most.

Some scholars think shepherds were looked down on in Jesus' time because they were unable to obey all the religious laws. Let the students share why they think God chose to announce His Son's birth to and through shepherds.

WHY GOD CHOOSES GRUNGY PEOPLE
(10 minutes)

Have a volunteer read 1 Corinthians 1:27–31. Ask, "What kind of people does God usually choose to carry out His will according to these verses?" List the answers (the foolish, the weak, the lowly, the despised) on newsprint or the board.

Ask the students to explain: "Why do you think God doesn't usually choose the wise, strong, high, and popular?" (One possibility: they might boast in themselves, thinking God chose them because they are better than others. God chooses us out of His goodness, not ours.) Ask, "What kind of people did Jesus hang out with?" Have the students think of the many "low-class" people among Jesus' crowd: fishermen, tax collectors, prostitutes, thieves, rebels, Samaritans, lepers, and the like. List these on the board or newsprint.

IT'S NOT JUST A JOB
(5 minutes)

Say, "God doesn't save or stay with you because of your human greatness, but because of His divine love for you." Allow students to respond to the first question on the student page. Encourage them to discover that even in the worst job God is present and cares for us because of His love for us, as shown by Jesus.

Say, "The shepherds brought glory to God by praising Him and telling others what they had seen as they returned to their work." Then discuss the second question. Student answers will vary, but may include sharing Christ with co-workers and keeping a positive attitude.

QUITTING TIME
(5 minutes)

Have the students each write a short prayer to God, thanking Him for, and asking for His help with, their work. Ask volunteers to share the prayers they wrote as a closing for the class.

LESSON EXTENDER

✝ Many suggest that a large number of new jobs in the future will be in "service industries"—heath care, social work, and hotels and restaurants. What characteristics are necessary for these jobs? How can these jobs be avenues of Christian witness?

✝ Write notes of appreciation to those who serve in your church—custodians, secretaries, and volunteers.

FROM GRUNGE to GLORY

THE WORST WORK
Describe the worst job or chore you ever had to do. What made it so awful?

....
....
....
....

Was there anything at all good about it?

....
....
....
....

OUT STANDING IN THEIR FIELD
Read **Luke 2:8–20**. What part of being a shepherd would you have hated most?

____ Handling smelly, oily, stupid animals

____ Being on duty twenty-four hours a day, almost year-round

____ Living in a field and sleeping on the ground

____ Working by yourself or with a few family members

____ Having to entertain yourself or be totally bored

Why do you suppose God chose to first announce His Son's birth to lowly shepherds?

____ Because their self-esteem needed boosting

____ Because they would have receptive hearts

____ Because the Good News was for *all* people

____ Because Jesus would be the Good Shepherd

____ Because _____

WHY GOD CHOOSES GRUNGY PEOPLE
Read **1 Corinthians 1:27–31**. Whom does God usually choose to carry out His will according to these verses? Why?

....
....
....

What kind of people did Jesus hang out with?

....
....
....

IT'S NOT JUST A JOB
What does God's love mean in the middle of a rotten job?

....

How can you bring glory to God even when you've still got grungy work to do?

....

Journey of Faith © 2007 Concordia Publishing House. Reproduced by permission.

STUDENT PAGE 7

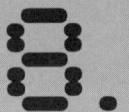 8. GODLY ROLE MODELS

Luke 2:21–40

Lesson Focus

Through the story of our newly born Savior being presented at the temple, students will consider how God's people were used to fulfill the Law and the prophecies about Jesus the Savior. Students are encouraged to see how the godly role models the Lord has placed in their lives help them know their Savior.

OPENING (5 minutes)

Discuss these questions with the students: What is a role model? Do you have role models? If so, who are they, and why did you choose them? Do you think most young people have role models? Why or why not?

GODLY MODELS OF THE PAST (20 minutes)

Distribute copies of the student page. Divide students into three groups, and assign one section to each group. Direct students to read the verses from Luke and then answer the questions in order to summarize and share their discoveries with the rest of the group. Guide students to see these points:

Joseph and Mary: They obeyed the Jewish law requiring them to circumcise a male child at eight days old as a reminder of God's covenant to Abraham; they consecrated their firstborn male to God as a reminder of how God saved Israel's firstborn males during the Passover. They offered the proper purification rites for a woman who gave birth to a son. Their obedience to each specific detail of these laws shows dedication to and faith in God.

Simeon: He was obviously very familiar with Scripture. His words about Jesus as a "light" for the Gentiles were not acceptable to all who heard it. Many Jewish people did not know, or they ignored, the reality that God would offer salvation to those outside their nation.

Anna: We know nothing about Anna's personal life except what these passages say. The words she shares give hope to those who look forward to God's promised Redeemer.

ABOUT GODLY ROLE MODELS (10 minutes)

Ask three volunteers to read the passages aloud. Discuss the questions as a whole group. Answers include faithfulness in the Lord, living as Christ would live, modeling faith and patience, speaking the Word of God, and faithfulness to the Lord.

GODLY ROLE MODELS OF THE PRESENT (20 minutes)

Say, "Because of Jesus, your parents are no longer bound by Jewish religious laws as they teach you about salvation in Him. How have they 'honored God' in the ways they have raised you?" Allow time for students to answer. Direct them to the questions on the student page. Have students consider how those other than parents and church staff have made an impact.

Provide markers and a sheet of poster paper titled "Our Godly Role Models." Ask students to list one or two of their present role models on the poster. Have students share their choices, guiding them in describing how they see these people live out their faith in Jesus Christ.

CLOSING (5 minutes)

Close with a prayer of thanksgiving for the spiritual role models your students have in their lives.

LESSON EXTENDER

✝ Optional opening: Have youth create a poster of the world's role models. Bring in magazines, and have students cut and paste pictures of role models onto a poster board. Before the closing, compare this with the "Our Godly Role Models" poster.

✝ Read 1 Timothy 4:12 and discuss young people's role as an "example." Who might imitate their faith?

20

GODLY ROLE MODELS

GODLY MODELS OF THE PAST

Joseph and Mary: **Luke 2:21–24**

Look at the following passages and discuss the Jewish (Old Testament) laws that Joseph and Mary fulfilled: Compare **verse 21** with **Genesis 17:9–14**.

....

Compare **verses 22–23** with **Exodus 13:1, 14–16**.

....

Compare **verse 24** with **Leviticus 12:1–4, 6–8**.

....

What do you learn about Joseph and Mary through their actions?

....

....

Simeon: **Luke 2:25–35**

Describe the kind of person Simeon was.

....

Compare **verses 29–32** with **Isaiah 9:2; 49:6**. What does this tell you about Simeon's understanding of the Old Testament Scriptures? Would all Jews in the temple be glad to hear these words?

....

....

Anna: **Luke 2:36–38**

Describe the kind of person Anna was.

....

Compare **verse 38** with **Psalm 130:7–8** and **Isaiah 59:20**. How do you think Anna knew that Jesus was the fulfillment of God's desire to redeem His people?

....

....

ABOUT GODLY ROLE MODELS

Read the following passages to discover what Scripture says we should imitate from the lives of Christians:

1 Corinthians 4:15–17

....

Hebrew 6:12

....

Hebrews 13:7

....

GODLY ROLE MODELS OF THE PRESENT

Who has God placed in your life to nurture your faith?

....

Who do you know that, like Simeon, knows and speaks God's Word clearly?

....

Who do you know that, like Anna, spends their days serving God and speaking words of hope to other people?

....

Journey of Faith © 2007 Concordia Publishing House. Reproduced by permission.

9. THE GREATEST GIFT

Matthew 2:1–12

Lesson Focus

Participants will see that our response to God for His gift of Jesus Christ is worship, praise, and thanksgiving.

THE BEST GIFT (10 minutes)

Distribute copies of the student page. Ask students to complete the questions. Have students talk about their best gift and how they responded to the gift giver.

WE THREE KINGS AND HEROD TOO (20 minutes)

Have students open to the text and ask a volunteer to read it aloud. Discuss the first question in this section. Lead students to see that the focus of the Wise Men's visit was to worship Jesus.

Share with students the following about King Herod: Herod was paranoid, jealous, and insecure. He was a tyrant who heavily taxed his subjects. Of his ten wives, he killed his favorite, as well as her grandfather, mother, two brothers-in-law (one of them the High Priest), and three of his sons. In his book *First Christmas*, Paul Maier quotes Herod's friend Augustus as saying, "I'd rather be Herod's pig than his son." Ask students why they think Herod wanted to eliminate Jesus. Possible answers include fear, jealousy, suspicion, insanity, and lack of faith.

In verse 8, Herod suggests to the Wise Men that he wanted to find Jesus and worship Him. Discuss with the students why it is difficult to worship someone you fear or don't trust.

Contrast Herod's response with that of the Wise Men. Note the joyful enthusiasm that sent the Wise Men in search of Jesus (verse 10). Verse 11 indicates that the Wise Men first worshiped Jesus and then gave Him gifts. Discuss with students the last two questions in this section.

MY GIFT OF WORSHIP (20 minutes)

Herod didn't recognize God's great gift because of his sin and lack of faith. The Wise Men recognized that Jesus was special but may not have known how special He was. Believers know how special a gift Jesus was. Have students think again about the best gift they ever received. How does it compare to God's gift to us in Jesus Christ? Allow students to reflect for a moment and then respond briefly.

Spend some time allowing students to answer the question about their response to God's gift of salvation.

One of the most important ways God allows us to express our response to Him is through our praise and worship. Ask students to rate their worship using the scale on the student page. The line represents a continuum. Encourage honesty. Take care not to judge students. Remind students that each person's experience will probably be distinct from others'.

Have students complete questions and share their responses.

CLOSING (5 minutes)

Have the students pair up and share their response plan with their partner. Have students close with prayer.

LESSON EXTENDER

✝ Ask students to hold one another accountable for the steps they indicated.

✝ Work with students and the pastor to plan a student-led worship service or suggest ways that students can be more involved in worship.

The Greatest Gift

THE BEST GIFT

What are the top three gifts you have ever received?

Which gift was the best? Why?

What are the three best gifts you have ever given?

Which was the best? Why?

How did you respond to the gift giver? What were your feelings toward him or her?

WE THREE KINGS AND HEROD TOO

Read **Matthew 2:1–12**.

Why did the Wise Men come seeking the king of the Jews (**verse 2**)?

What was Herod's problem? Why did he want to eliminate Jesus (**verse 3**)?

Why do you think Herod couldn't truly worship Jesus (**verses 7–8**)?

What were the Wise Men's gifts an indication of?

Which do you think was greater, the Wise Men's worship or their gifts? Why (**verses 9–11**)?

MY GIFT OF WORSHIP

Consider the best gift you ever received and your response to the giver. How much greater is God's gift to you in Jesus Christ?

How do you respond to God's gift of salvation through His Son, Jesus Christ?

Rate your worship using the scale below by placing a letter for each of the following on the line.

I'm Going through the Motions _____ *Is Church Over Already?*

C—Confession   S—Singing   P—Praying   L—Listening   O—Offering

Why is God worthy to be worshiped?

What hinders you in your worship?

What helps you in your worship?

What role does the Gospel message of salvation through faith in Jesus play in our attitude and action of worship?

What are three intentional steps can you take to enhance your worship?

STUDENT PAGE 9

Journey of Faith © 2007 Concordia Publishing House. Reproduced by permission.

10. THE HOLY REFUGEE FAMILY

Matthew 2:13–23

Lesson Focus

In many ways, God cares for those who, like Jesus' family, are refugees because of violence and oppression.

THINKING ABOUT THE ISSUE (10 minutes)

Distribute copies of the student page. Have students answer the questions in the opening activity. After all have had time to complete the activity, share the following correct answers: A = 15 million; B = true (see Matthew 2:13–23); C = they *all* were (there are also many others in the Bible); D = false (it's Lutheran Immigration and Refugee Service, an LCMS World Relief partner organization); E = true (see Numbers 35:9–15); F = true (see Matthew 8:20). Ask students what conclusions they draw from this exercise. The existence of refugees worldwide is a critical issue for people who care, especially Christians. How can we respond?

JESUS WAS A REFUGEE (20 minutes)

Have a student read Matthew 2:13–23 to the class. Then direct students' attention to the second section of the student page. As you discuss several or all of the following questions, encourage students to write notes on the student page. Challenge students to be as thorough, thoughtful, and articulate in their responses as possible.

A. Why did Jesus and His family become refugees? (Under threat of violence from Herod)

B. For what reasons might people become refugees? (Famine, war, disease, natural disasters, religious persecution, government breakdown)

C. Are there refugee families in your neighborhood, community, church, or school? Do you know where they are from? (Responses will vary; recent refugees might be from Cuba, Sudan, or Kosovo.)

D. How can refugees today know that God understands their plight and will provide the help they need? (By being served by Christians who really care for them; by hearing the Good News of God's love for all people)

E. What do you think the needs of a refugee include? What would you need if you were a refugee? (Shelter; food; clothing; compassion; how to deal with the language barrier; how to figure out daily rules, regulations, and expectations; how to figure out systems in the new community, such as the legal system, the educational system, the medical system, and the welfare system)

F. How can you help the refugees you know? How does knowing that Jesus and His family were refugees encourage you to help? (See Matthew 25:40. We can help others because of our commitment of faith; we can respond to any need, by ourselves or with others; we can tell them about Refugee Jesus.)

G. What kinds of jobs might a person pursue if he or she wants to work in an adult career to help refugees, immigrants, and similarly hurting people? (Responses will vary.)

SERVE THEM, SERVE ME! (15 minutes)

Invite a student to read Matthew 25:31–40 to the class. Then encourage the class to respond to the statements on the student page. Allow students time to share their responses with one another.

CLOSING (5 minutes)

Read Isaiah 1:16–17 and Deuteronomy 24:19–21. Then pray together, asking God for power, encouragement, and opportunity to seek the welfare of others, including the displaced and the dispossessed.

THE HOLY REFUGEE FAMILY

THINKING ABOUT THE ISSUE
Answer the following by circling the correct answers.

A. According to U.N. statistics, in the past ten years there has been an annual average of how many million refugees worldwide?
5, 10, 15, 20, 25, or 30 million

B. Jesus and His family were refugees for a time. **true or false**

C. Which of the following were refugees or displaced persons at some time in their lives? **Adam and Eve, Cain, Abraham, Jacob, Joseph (son of Jacob), Moses, Ruth, David, Jeremiah, Mary and Joseph, Jesus, Paul**

D. There is no Lutheran organization that helps refugees and immigrants. **true or false**

E. God provided cities of refuge in Old Testament Israel. **true or false**

F. Jesus really said, "The Son of Man has no place to lay His head." **true or false**

JESUS WAS A REFUGEE
I never knew that . . .

....

I think this means . . .

....

I am changed by . . .

....

SERVE THEM, SERVE ME!
After reading **Matthew 25:31–40**, complete the following statements.

If I really believe that doing something to meet the need(s) of a hurting person is the same as doing it to Jesus, I will . . .

....

The one thing I really remember about helping someone else is . . .

....

"Do to others," "Love the Lord your God with all your heart," and "Love your neighbor as yourself" mean to me that . . .

....

When I read the phrase "Jesus became a refugee from heaven for me," I think or feel . . .

....

Because of my sin, I was a refugee. God's grace in Christ Jesus makes me a citizen of the kingdom of heaven and promises a wonderful home for me in glory. This makes me feel . . .

....

Journey of Faith © 2007 Concordia Publishing House. Reproduced by permission.

11. Family Matters

Luke 2:41–52;
Hebrews 2:10–18

Lesson Focus

Teens today are being bombarded with views of family that are far different from God's. In this session they will compare two families (their earthly family and their heavenly family) as they look at the life of Jesus.

OPENING (10 minutes)

Today there are many television sitcoms portraying different types of families. Have the students discuss several of them. How do they portray relationships between parents? difficulties of one-parent families? teens living in a household with no parental guidance? children being raised by someone other than a parent?

YOUR EARTHLY FAMILY (7 minutes)

Distribute copies of the student page. Have students consider what they would like to see in their earthly families by completing the first section. Discuss their answers.

YOUR HEAVENLY FAMILY (8 minutes)

Now have students complete the set of questions for their heavenly family. They will have to adjust their thinking, since they are not the head of this family, but are instead one of the children.

Discuss their answers. Tell the students that they will see both types of families in the life of the twelve-year-old Jesus.

FAMILY FOUNDATIONS (15 minutes)

Read Luke 2:41–52 aloud. A growing number of children today have two fathers. Jesus' situation was different. His earthly father, Joseph (called "a parent" and "your father" in Luke 2), was not His birth parent. God Himself, through the Holy Spirit, conceived Him and was His true heavenly Father. Ask the students to share their answers to the questions on the student page. (Mary and Joseph searched for Jesus until they found Him. Jesus' trip to Jerusalem fulfilled the obligation of the Law, but it also became an opportunity for Him to begin to teach the truth of the Scriptures to the teachers in the temple.)

BRINGING IT HOME (10 minutes)

Read Hebrews 2:10–18 together. Allow students time to answer the questions on the student page. Encourage volunteers to share their answers. Spend time reviewing the words of verses 14–18. Help students see Christ's role in their salvation. (We are of the same family as Jesus, according to verse 11. Because Christ shared in our humanity, we share in His death and resurrection. It is because of His perfect keeping of the Law that we are declared righteous.)

CLOSING (5 minutes)

Lead the class in prayer, thanking God for families. Be sure to include a prayer of thanksgiving for the saving work of Jesus.

LESSON EXTENDER

✝ Refer to Matthew 12:46–50 and John 19:25–27 to see how Jesus responded to each of His families.

Family Matters

YOUR EARTHLY FAMILY

How old do you want to be when you get married? _____

Will you want children? _____

How old do you want to be when you have your first child?
_____

How many children would you like? _____

Put these qualities in the order that you would like to see them in your children (1—most important; 8—least important).

___ Respectful of authority ___ Good-looking

___ Having a good attitude ___ God-loving

___ Smart ___ Obedient

___ Healthy ___ Athletic

YOUR HEAVENLY FAMILY

How did you become a member of God's heavenly family?

....
....

What is your role in the heavenly family?

....
....

What qualities do children of God have?

....
....

FAMILY FOUNDATIONS

Read **Luke 2:41–52**. List the things mentioned that showed Jesus had a loving and caring family here on earth.

....
....

What actions and words of Jesus tell us about His earthly and heavenly families?

....
....

What responsibilities to His heavenly Father and His earthly parents did Jesus carry out on this trip to Jerusalem?

....
....

BRINGING IT HOME

Read **Hebrews 2:10–18**. What are we told about our relationship with Jesus? **(verse 11)**

....

Look closely at **verses 14–18**. What words tell us how much God cares for us? What has Christ done for us? Give examples of Jesus' human and divine natures from these verses.

....

Journey of Faith © 2007 Concordia Publishing House. Reproduced by permission.

STUDENT PAGE 11

12. Preparing God's Way

Malachi 3:1–4;
Philippians 1:3–11;
Luke 3:1–6

Lesson Focus

Teens may overlook the impact of their Christian witness upon their peers. This lesson reaffirms them as instruments of the Holy Spirit in preparing the way of Christ in the lives of others.

OPENING (5 minutes)

Discuss: In what way is the relationship of the advertising executive to producer, performer to songwriter, and ambassador to president similar to the relationship between the messenger and the source? Where else does this happen? What Bible stories describe how God brought people to faith? Ask the students to tell about when Christ first came into their lives. Who were the messengers of God's grace? What was the process? How do friends, parents, teachers, pastors, Holy Baptism, the Bible, church, and youth groups each influence their faith?

(This lesson builds on the premise that infant Baptism is a powerful way that Christ enters life through water and the Word. The Holy Spirit may often use events and other people as instruments that prepare someone's heart to receive the Gospel.)

PREPARING THE WAY (10 minutes)

Have students complete the matching activity on the student page. Prepare slips of paper that include a Bible reference about Gospel messengers on the inside fold and the student's name on the outside. These verses may include Matthew 28:18–20; John 3:5; John 3:14–15; John 3:16–18; Romans 8:16–17; Romans 8:37–39; Romans 10:8–15; Ephesians 2:8–10; Philippians 1:9–11; and 1 John 1:8–9. Have the students read aloud their Bible reference and briefly express what their passage says about the message or the messenger. Who is the messenger? What is the message? These verses contain God's message to them of His love and forgiveness. The means of grace—God's Word and Sacraments—proclaim God's message with power. Any teacher or evangelist or servant merely serves as a messenger of God's love and forgiveness.

LOOKING INTO THE MESSAGE (20 minutes)

The church season of Advent is a time of preparation and expectation. Malachi 3:1–4 talks of a God-sent messenger who would prepare the way for the Messiah. Luke 3:1–6 shows the fulfillment of this prophesy through John the Baptizer. He was sent from God as a divine messenger to prepare people for Jesus, calling them to repentance for the forgiveness of sins (Luke 3:3). Help students learn more about the messenger and his message. Read Malachi 3:1–4 and Luke 3:1–6 to complete the questions from the student page.

SHARING THE MESSAGE (10 minutes)

Help the students see how they have been graciously called by the Gospel of Jesus Christ and claimed by the waters of Baptism. In Holy Baptism they have been marked as disciples of Christ to be His witnesses, His messengers. The work of God's messengers has not changed: it is to share God's message of salvation with others, preparing the way for Jesus to touch their lives. Let the students finish their section on "Sharing the Message."

CLOSING (5 minutes)

Remind the students that God's messengers bring *God's* message, not their own. If a person rejects the messenger, then they are really rejecting God. Invite the students to pray that the Holy Spirit would use them as His messengers to share God's message about sin and grace with others.

LESSON EXTENDER

✝ Encourage the students to make a prayer list including their friends, classmates, workmates, or family members who need the life-changing power of Jesus' grace. Encourage them to identify specific ways that the Holy Spirit would use them as His messengers.

PREPARING GOD'S WAY

PREPARING THE WAY
Match each occupation with the most accurate description.

1. A teacher about a situation
2. A weatherman
3. A messenger to him
4. A reporter
5. A preacher on a subject
6. An anchorman to another

a. shares a personal interview.
b. proclaims God's Word.
c. publicly shares the news channeled.
d. warns of an approaching storm front.
e. instructs others with information.
f. delivers special news from one person.

LOOKING INTO THE MESSAGE

In **Malachi 3:1** . . .

Who is the Sender?

....

Whose message was to be proclaimed?

....

What was to be the work of the messenger?

....

In **Luke 3:1–6** . . .

Who was God's promised messenger?

....

In what location did he share the message?

....

What was this message?

....

What was the purpose for this messenger and this message?

....

Has the purpose changed any today? Why or why not?

....

What is the heart of the Gospel message? When is it most difficult to share? What might make it easier to be a messenger?

....

SHARING THE MESSAGE
Someone I know who needs Jesus is

....

Some excuses that person has for not wanting to be part of God's family or the Church are . . .

....

I can be God's messenger to this person by . . .

....

....

....

....

As a messenger of God, when I read **Philippians 1:9–11**, I . . .

....

....

....

....

Journey of Faith © 2007 Concordia Publishing House. Reproduced by permission.

STUDENT PAGE 12

13. Be Radical

Luke 3:15–17, 21–22

Lesson Focus

Jesus, our Savior, loves and forgives us radically so we can live out our faith, loving others too.

EXPECTATIONS AND BEING RADICAL
(5 minutes)

After distributing copies of the student page, engage students in a discussion about how expectations relate to peer pressure. The opposite of going along with peer pressure is perhaps behaving in unexpected ways.

Then, encourage students to think in general terms. If they were to encounter someone claiming to be a prophet or the Son of God, what would they expect? Prophets are generally considered those who foretell the future or tell about God. Have your students imagine what it must have been like to be a first-century Jew. It would be natural to assume that the Son of God would be powerful, wealthy, political, and so forth.

JOHN THE BAPTIZER, A RADICAL PROPHET
(15 minutes)

Encourage students to work together in breakout groups to read the suggested texts and answer the questions. Discuss the eccentricities of John the Baptizer. He ate locusts and wore camel's hair. Ask students, "If you saw someone behaving like John today, what would you think?" Although the people weren't sure whether John was the Christ or not, John always pointed to the Savior coming after him.

JESUS, THE RADICAL SAVIOR (20 minutes)

Make a list with the students about how Jesus behaved differently than expected. Jesus lowered Himself to take on human form (John 1:14; Colossians 2:9); He was born a poor, homeless refugee (2 Corinthians 8:9; Matthew 8:20); and He grew up as a humble carpenter's son (unlike Moses, who grew up in Pharaoh's palace).

OUR RADICAL FAITH
(5 minutes)

Although we deserve eternal death for our sin, God's Son died on the cross for us, thus demonstrating His radical love for all of humanity.

Encourage students to think about being "radical" themselves in living out their faith among their friends and peers. Not attending parties where drugs are sold and indulged in; abstaining from premarital sex; telling their friends about their faith: all these are ways in which Christian teens can show a radical faith.

Close in prayer, asking for trust in God's radical promises and for opportunities to share our radical faith with others.

LESSON EXTENDER

✞ Challenge students to think of other Bible characters who were "radical" in their proclamation of the Good News about Jesus. Examples might include the conversion of Paul (Acts 22); the bold demonstration of faith by Abraham at Mount Moriah (Genesis 22); or the martyrdom of Stephen (Acts 7).

✞ If time allows, consider reviewing the questions and answers on "The Two Natures of Jesus Christ" in Luther's Small Catechism (questions 118–124). While Jesus humbled Himself to manhood, He still was true God at the same time.

Be Radical

EXPECTATIONS AND BEING RADICAL
How would you describe peer pressure? What is the opposite of going along with peer pressure?

How would you expect a prophet to behave?

How would you expect the Son of God to behave?

JOHN THE BAPTIZER, A RADICAL PROPHET
Read **Matthew 3:4–6**. How did John dress? What did he eat? What is unexpected about this?

Read **Luke 3:15–17, 21–22**. As a prophet, what did John proclaim?

What did the people expect of him? (See **verse 15**.)

Did he try to draw attention to himself? (See **verse 16**.)

JESUS, THE RADICAL SAVIOR
How was Jesus different from what might be expected from a royal heir?

Describe John's statement in **Luke 3:16**. How is he different from Jesus?

How did Jesus hide His power and authority? (See **Philippians 2:5–11**.)

What does Paul say about how the world will view Christ (**1 Corinthians 1:18–25**)?

OUR RADICAL FAITH
What do we deserve because of our sins (**Matthew 10:28**)?

What was Jesus' ultimate sacrifice in demonstrating His radical love (**Mark 10:45**)?

Rejoicing in the forgiveness shown to us in Christ, we can live out our faith radically, rejecting the world and embracing God. Make a list of some ways you might surprise expectations as a Christian.

Journey of Faith © 2007 Concordia Publishing House. Reproduced by permission.

STUDENT PAGE 13

14. TROUNCING TEMPTATION

Matthew 4:1–11; 8:23–27

Lesson Focus

Although Satan, the world, and our own sinful nature tempt us, God provides the model (Jesus) and the weapon (His Word) that enable us to effectively fight temptation

INTRODUCTION (5 minutes)

Divide the class into small groups of two or three. Tell each group to discuss the question "What do you think is the most common temptation for the average person living today?" After no more than three minutes, have each group share their answer. Today's lesson will talk about temptations and how God helps us fight those temptations and live to His glory instead.

TARGETING TEMPTATIONS (20 minutes)

Distribute copies of the student page. Remind the students that temptations plague people of every age. Have groups discuss common temptations of the age groups listed. Briefly have each group share their responses. Have the group discuss what three temptations might be greatest for youth today.

Point out that, although the temptations might change, both the internal and external pressures are constant for every generation. Satan never gives up trying to sway people from Christ. The world continues to lure Christians to participate in sinful activities. Our human nature has been inclined to sin since the time of Adam and Eve. Dealing with temptation is common to every age in every culture.

RATIONALIZING THE REALITY (10 minutes)

Ask students to define the word rationalize ("to devise self-satisfying but incorrect reasons for one's behavior"). Explain that when people rationalize, they are simply making excuses for their behavior.

After discussing rationalizations teens might use today, read Matthew 4:1–11. Discuss the questions on the student page. People often feel that Jesus had resources that aren't available to mere humans. Ask the class to identify the weapon Jesus used to battle Satan and temptation. Is this weapon available to humans today?

RECOGNIZING OUR RELIEF (10 minutes)

Discuss the questions and the blessings that are ours when temptations are overcome using God's power. Have the students read Matthew 8:23–27 and discuss the questions from the student page. Remind the class that even though technology helps us to predict the weather, we cannot yet control it. Jesus was so powerful, however, He could control the weather with His word alone. Discuss the promise of 1 Corinthians 10:13 as Jesus' power at work in your life.

CLOSING (5 minutes)

Close with a group prayer thanking God for Jesus' victory over sin, death, and the devil. Allow students to include petitions for special temptations or needs that they may have.

LESSON EXTENDER

✝ Challenge the class to find Bible verses that speak to the temptations they identified in the Targeting Temptations section. Some students might write a devotion based upon a particular verse to overcome a specific temptation.

✝ Discuss how the world makes temptations appealing (consider TV shows, movies, music, etc.). Ask students to evaluate whether Christians should allow themselves to be exposed to the world's temptations. If not, what can young people do about the situation?

Trouncing Temptation

TARGETING TEMPTATIONS
Identify common temptations for . . .

elementary school students

....

high school students

....

college students

....

parents

....

senior citizens

....

What are the most common temptations youth in your community face?

....

RATIONALIZING THE REALITY
What are some common rationalizations people have for giving in to temptation?

....

....

Satan is the master of rationalizations. He even threw rationalizations at Jesus. Read **Matthew 4:1–11**. Can you spot the devil's rationalizations?

....

....

Had He been inclined to sin, what rationalizations might Jesus have used when faced with these temptations?

....

....

Instead of rationalizing, how did Jesus respond? What "weapon" did He use?

....

....

RECOGNIZING OUR RELIEF
What was the end result of Jesus' refusal to give in to Satan's temptations?

....

....

....

What promise does this hold for us when we are tempted?

....

....

....

Jesus has more power than just the ability to say no to the devil. Read **Matthew 8:23–27**. What do these verses tell about Jesus' power?

....

....

....

Read **1 Corinthians 10:13**. How does God's power help us?

....

....

STUDENT PAGE 14

Journey of Faith © 2007 Concordia Publishing House. Reproduced by permission.

15. Calling All Sinners

Mark 2:13–17

Lesson Focus

Jesus calls us to repent and receive His free gifts.

FAME (10 minutes)

Begin the session with the following questions to help break into the topic: Have you ever met anyone slightly or really famous? How did they respond to you? How did their interest or disinterest in you affect you? Allow time for students to share their answers.

AN UNLIKELY CANDIDATE (20 minutes)

Give copies of the student page to each participant. Read Mark 2:13–17. Levi, also called Matthew, had most likely heard of Jesus' miracles and teachings before He passed by on this day. As a tax collector, Matthew was the lowest of the low—a bloodsucker, a cheat, a traitor. He had hardened himself against the insults hurled at him. What was it, then, that made Matthew drop everything and follow Jesus? (Jesus worked faith in his heart and took interest in him regardless of his reputation and position.) What was Matthew's response? (He invited Jesus to his house; Luke tells us it was a great banquet [Luke 5:29]; he became a devoted disciple.) What is at the heart of the Pharisees' complaint? (Envy. If Jesus was so important, why wasn't He spending time with important people?) Does Jesus' answer imply that there are some people who do not need repentance and forgiveness? Why or why not? (No, the Pharisees only thought they were healthier than they actually were. Only those who realize their sinfulness can comprehend their need for a Savior.)

A CLOSER LOOK (15 minutes)

Have students work in groups of two or three to answer the questions in this section. Allow time for small groups to share their insights with the whole group. Why is it sometimes hard to believe that God's grace could be extended to the "lowest of the low"? (Human beings measure, or rank, evil, but God does not. A little evil is still evil in God's eyes, and all people need both repentance and forgiveness.) What does it mean to "repent"? (Sorrow for and a desire to turn away from sin. This is not a onetime event for God's people. Daily we sin much, repent, and receive His forgiveness.) Matthew did not follow Jesus secretly, as seen by the great banquet he gave. Why is it difficult, even impossible, to "follow" Jesus secretly? (Through the work of the Holy Spirit, repentance is cultivated in us and changes the way we think and act; it's a radical change that is often noticed by others.)

CLOSING (5 minutes)

Pray, "God in heaven, You have called all people to You. We confess we don't always act as Your people should. Help us to repent and turn back to You. May others see Your light shining in us and through us. In the name of the true light, Jesus. Amen."

LESSON EXTENDER

✝ Discuss as a group some ways that people show that they are following Jesus. Plan ways that you could together and individually demonstrate faith in Jesus.

Calling All Sinners

AN UNLIKELY CANDIDATE

Read **Mark 2:13–17**. Levi, also called Matthew, had most likely heard of Jesus' miracles and teachings before He passed by on this day. As a tax collector, Matthew was the lowest of the low—a bloodsucker, a cheat, a traitor. He had hardened himself against the insults hurled at him. What was it, then, that made Matthew drop everything and follow Jesus?

What was Matthew's response? (See also **Luke 5:27–32**.)

What is at the heart of the Pharisees' complaint?

Does Jesus' answer imply that there are some people who do not need repentance and forgiveness?

Why or why not?

A CLOSER LOOK

Why is it sometimes hard to believe that God's grace could be extended to the "lowest of the low"?

What does it mean to "repent"?

Matthew did not follow Jesus secretly, as seen by the great banquet he gave. Why is it difficult, even impossible, to "follow" Jesus secretly?

Journey of Faith © 2007 Concordia Publishing House. Reproduced by permission.

STUDENT PAGE 15

16. Jesus Calls Disciples

John 1:43–51

Lesson Focus

As students interact with the text regarding Jesus' call of these two disciples, they will recognize that they have been called through Baptism.

OPENING (10 minutes)

Make copies of the skit below, and give them to the students who will portray the characters. Have the volunteers perform the skit for the rest of the class as an introduction to the lesson.

CALLING THE FIRST DISCIPLES (20 minutes)

Work through this section as a group. Ask a student to read aloud the Micah passage, but have all students look at Psalm 139. Lead them to understand the following:

Jesus finds Philip; Philip finds Nathanael and tells him that he has found the Messiah. It is significant that Jesus first finds Philip, for that is the way God works. He comes to us and enables us to know Him.

The way Nathanael asked his question implies that Nazareth was an unimportant place.

Jesus is God, and God knows all about us! It is comforting because God can care for us in every situation. It may be disconcerting to realize that He also knows all of the sinful thoughts and actions that we would like to hide from Him.

Jesus is referring to Jacob's vision of a ladder reaching heaven in Genesis 28:12. He takes this scriptural picture and applies it to Himself. He is the mediator (ladder) between heaven and earth. Through His death and resurrection He reconnects God and man.

CALLING DISCIPLES TODAY (10 minutes)

Allow students to answer the questions before looking up the Thessalonians passages. Refer to the Baptism collage from last week to help students understand that they were called at their Baptism.

BEING A DISCIPLE OF CHRIST (10 minutes)

Discuss answers to the first question together. Encourage students to answer the remaining questions on their own and take the quiet prayer time seriously. Ask for volunteers to close in prayer or pray aloud yourself asking that God will enable students to act on their roles as disciples this week.

Jesus Calls Disciples—A Skit

Setting: Jesus and two or three disciples are walking, Philip is standing a short distance away. Nathanael is sitting even farther away studying Scripture under a fig tree. The story begins as Jesus and His followers approach Philip.

Jesus: Philip, follow Me.

(Philip follows, then runs to find Nathanael. Jesus and the disciples sit down in a circle as if Jesus is teaching them.)

Philip: *(excitedly)* We have found the one Moses wrote about in the Law, and about whom the prophets also wrote—Jesus of Nazareth, the son of Joseph.

Nathanael: Nazareth! Can anything good come from there?

Philip: Come and see.
(Philip and Nathanael walk toward Jesus)

Jesus: *(speaks to disciples and points toward Nathanael)* Here is a true Israelite, in whom there is nothing false.

Nathanael: How do You know me?

Jesus: I saw you while you were still under the fig tree before Philip called you.

Nathanael: Rabbi, You are the Son of God; You are the King of Israel.

Jesus: You believe because I told you I saw you under the fig tree. You shall see greater things than that. I tell you the truth, you shall see heaven open, and the angels of God ascending and descending on the Son of Man.

Jesus Calls Disciples

You are invited to become a Disciple!

CALLING THE FIRST DISCIPLES

Refer to **John 1:43–51**.

Look over **verses 43–45**. How many times do you see the words finding and/or found? Who found whom first? Why is that significant?

Why might Nathanael be skeptical about the Messiah coming from Nazareth? How does **Matthew 2:23** shed light on his comment?

What does **Psalm 139:1–16** tell us about how Jesus knew what Nathanael was doing? Do you find this truth comforting or disturbing? Why?

What is Jesus referring to in **John 1:50–51**?

CALLING DISCIPLES TODAY

Do you think Jesus still calls persons to be His disciples? Look at **1 Thessalonians 2:11–12**; check **5:23–24** to verify your response.

BEING A DISCIPLE OF CHRIST

At Baptism God made you His child, called you His own, and clothed you with Christ. Now, through His Holy Spirit, God guides you to respond to His call that you be a disciple of Christ. Consider what you know about the actions of the New Testament disciples, and list ways that a disciple responds to God's call. Write down one way you might act on your role as a disciple this week.

Spend a few moments in silent prayer asking God to enable you to carry out the actions you wrote down.

Journey of Faith © 2007 Concordia Publishing House. Reproduced by permission.

STUDENT PAGE 16

17. Demons Defeated

Mark 1:21–28

Lesson Focus

As teens deal with real-life issues, Christ has power to fortify them against sin, death, and the devil.

OPENING (5 minutes)

Ask the students, "If Christ were to speak at your school in an assembly, what topics would He talk about? How might He keep your attention? What would give Him credibility?" After allowing volunteers to respond, point out that credibility is an issue in many of our contacts with others.

WHOM WOULD YOU TRUST? (10 minutes)

Distribute copies of the student page. Ask students to complete the exercise. Discuss how they rated the people and why.

Also ask, "Which is most important to you—a person's words or actions? Why?" Encourage discussion by affirming those willing to offer their opinions.

OPPONENTS (20 minutes)

Read Mark 1:21–28 as a group. (If you wish, you could have students role-play the Bible passage.) Then direct the students' attention to the chart on the student page. Working alone or in pairs, have them list ways in which Jesus and Satan and his demons oppose—that is, are opposites of—each other. While they work, recreate the chart on the board, on newsprint, or on an overhead transparency. After about five minutes, invite volunteers to share their responses and write them on your large chart. The responses may include sinful/sinless, pure/evil, God/less than God, loving/malicious, healing/harmful, saving/damning, and forgives sins/tempts us to sin.

Discuss the following questions:

1. Why was Jesus able to relieve the man in Mark 1 of demon possession? (Jesus is greater than Satan and his demons.)

2. What means did Jesus use to accomplish this? (Jesus' simple words, "Be quiet. Come out of him," were all that was required. Jesus was more than a terrific orator. His words had real power.)

3. Christ's words have the power to change and heal us, too. How can we be certain of that truth? (God arms us with His Word, the Bible, and His Sacraments, the Word given through the physical elements of Baptism and Holy Communion, as our power for a life that resists the devil and his forces.)

AVOIDING DEMONS (10 minutes)

Invite the students to read the explanatory text and mark the suggested responses in this section of the student page. Be sensitive to the level of trust in your group as you invite sharing. Students may be more willing to talk in generalities ("Some young people are involved in . . . ") rather than personally ("Satan tempts me to . . . ").

Invite students to suggest some specific ways they are strengthened to resist temptation. Some ways they may suggest include reassurance of forgiveness, Christian friends and mentors, Bible study, participation in worship, and prayer.

CLOSING (5 minutes)

Pray, asking that your students be strengthened to resist the devil and share the power of Christ in their lives.

LESSON EXTENDER

✢ Invite students to use Bible reference books to locate and record promises from God that will help them resist Satan.

✢ Use a concordance to locate Bible passages including the words *devil, Satan,* or *demons.* Study these verses in context to strengthen the students' understanding of these spiritual opponents and Christ's complete victory over them.

DEMONS DEFEATED

WHOM WOULD YOU TRUST?
Rank the following people from most trustworthy (1) to least trustworthy (9). Be ready to discuss reasons for your ranking.

___ Telephone salesperson

___ Pastor

___ Late-night talk-show host

___ Politician

___ Nun

___ Lawyer

___ MTV or Radio DJ

___ Your parent(s)

___ Well-educated professor

OPPONENTS
Read **Mark 1:21–28**. List at least four differences between Christ Jesus and Satan and his demons.

CHRIST	Satan and His Demons!

AVOIDING DEMONS
What are ways that you believe the devil might possess, tempt, and bring evil to you and others? Mark those that you think might apply today.

___ Temptations to smoking, drinking alcohol, or drug abuse

___ Skipping church/Bible Study

___ Listening to evil music

___ Satanism/Satan worship

___ Cheating in school

___ Sexual immorality and lust

___ Demon possession

___ Cults

___ Tarot cards, Ouija boards, séances, and the occult

___ Atheism

___ Other: _____

How can Christ free you from temptation to sin and the bondage of Satan?

....

....

....

....

STUDENT PAGE 17

Journey of Faith © 2007 Concordia Publishing House. Reproduced by permission.

18. A Battle of Wills

Mark 1:40–45

Lesson Focus

Trusting Jesus' gracious will, the leper was healed. By grace through faith in Christ's death and resurrection for the forgiveness of our sins, we have received the Holy Spirit, who helps us live according to God's will, not our own.

OPENING (5 minutes)

Before class, write the following words in a single column on a sheet of newsprint. Use a marker in the color indicated in parentheses: *Blue* (in red); *Green* (in yellow); *Red* (in blue); and *Yellow* (in green). Challenge students to see who can read these words the fastest. The brain wants to say the *color* in which the word was written instead of the word that is *printed!* Point out to the students that this "battle of the wills" is nothing compared with the battle of our sinful will against the good and gracious will of God for our lives.

GETTING INTO SCRIPTURE (15 minutes)

Distribute copies of the student page. Have the students read Mark 1:32–34 and then verse 40. Have the students reflect on how the leper approached Jesus using the questions on the student page. Especially note the use of the word *willing*. When we pray, God always wants us to ask for His will to be done. God's will is gracious, which means He *always* takes care of us—even though we don't deserve it!

GOING DEEPER (15 minutes)

Read Mark 1:41–42. Have the students answer the two questions about the Lord's response to the leper. Point out that Jesus said, "I am willing," and then He *touched* this outcast from society, showing God's love for everyone. With His Word, Jesus heals the man. Through that same Word—beginning in our Baptism—the Holy Spirit gives us saving faith in Jesus whereby we receive the forgiveness He won through His crucifixion and resurrection.

In Mark 1:43–45, the man disobeys Jesus' clear instructions, and Jesus cannot minister freely in the cities. Even though we, like this man, may *think* we know what's best, trusting God means we seek to have our will "match" God's will. This "matching" of wills only happens through the power of God's Holy Spirit as He teaches us through His Word!

PONDERING THE GOSPEL (15 minutes)

Read the student page comments and invite responses.

Examples might include our curfew and other rules/expectations. They may include tension with a brother, sister, or friend who only sees something their way. The worst is putting our selfish will in front of God's will for us. The Bible calls this behavior "sin."

In gratitude to God we acknowledge that He "works in [us] to will and to act according to His good purpose," in "everything without complaining or arguing" (Philippians 2:13–14).

Invite the students to include these prayer thoughts in the closing.

CLOSING (5 minutes)

Invite the students to take turns praying, including thoughts they would like to share. Ask God for forgiveness when our will goes against His and give Him thanks for His gracious will for us in Christ.

LESSON EXTENDER

✝ See Matthew 26:36–46. Though our Lord had the power to escape the cross, whose will alone did He seek?

✝ See James 4:13–17. Before checking our daily planning calendar, which "Daily Planner" do we need to consult first in prayer before doing the day's business?

A Battle of Wills

GETTING INTO SCRIPTURE
Read **Mark 1:32–34** and then **Mark 1:40**. No doubt this leper had heard of the healing miracles Jesus had performed for many others. How did this leper introduce himself to Jesus in his body language?

....

in his spoken language?

....

GOING DEEPER
Next read **Mark 1:41–42**. How did our Lord respond to this leper

in His body language?

....

in His spoken language?

....

Now read **Mark 1:43–45**. What new battle of wills did the former leper now face

with what Jesus wanted him to do?

....

with what he wanted to do?

....

PONDERING THE GOSPEL
Share your reflections on the thoughts below.

Where do we find ourselves in a battle of wills with our parents, with our brothers, sisters, friends, . . . with God?

....

When we fight these battles, who are we looking out for?

....

What does the Bible call that behavior?

....

Today's Good News is that God's will is always looking after what is best in our lives! Jesus proved His unselfish love by touching and healing the leper, but mostly by His death on the cross, which heals us all from the guilt and punishment we deserve for our sins. See **Philippians 2:13–16a**. How does God help us show our gratitude to Him in Christ when we feel our will battling His?

....

Write one or two prayer thoughts in which you ask God to help you in areas where your will is battling His.

....

....

Journey of Faith © 2007 Concordia Publishing House. Reproduced by permission.

19. THE REAL DEAL

Mark 2:1–12

Lesson Focus

Through Christ, God still brings His Kingdom into the lives of young people today and helps them know His forgiveness and healing presence.

WHICH ONE IS REAL? (10 minutes)

Distribute copies of the student page. Have students guess the correct meaning of each word in the opening activity. Have volunteers share which definition they chose and why. (The correct answers are 1—b; 2—a; 3—b.)

Say, "It was hard to guess the real meaning of these words, especially when three or four definitions sounded pretty good. Today, we hear many definitions of 'really living.' Many of them may sound pretty good. How can we choose the right one?"

PROMISES, PROMISES (20 minutes)

Invite the students to share their responses to the three questions. (In a larger class, you may wish to do this in groups of three or four.) Have some samples and personal examples ready to "prime the pump."

Point out that we all hate broken promises. Friends fail us. Products don't live up to their advertising. Promised gifts don't arrive. These broken promises hurt. They also make us wary of being hurt again. That mood may have prevailed among the Jews when Jesus came proclaiming that the kingdom of God was at hand.

Read the Bible passages and discuss the questions. Suggested responses are as follows:

1. John's disciples were looking for the Messiah, the one who was promised to save Israel.
2. The proof Jesus offered was the fulfillment of the signs that the Old Testament prophesied would accompany the coming of the Kingdom (such as Isaiah 35:4–6). These signs were proof of God's power and presence in Jesus.
3. Jesus miraculously healed the paralytic man. One purpose of Jesus' miracles was to demonstrate that He was divine with the power and authority to heal, not just the body, but the spirit as well. He performed miracles, not just for healing, but to demonstrate the life-giving power of salvation and the forgiveness of sins.
4. God alone can forgive sins. Jesus here forgives sins, proving that He is God.

CHOOSE WHAT'S REAL (15 minutes)

Read the opening paragraph of this section. Then discuss the question. Point out that some young people look for support in things like sports, popularity, "stuff," physical appearance, and boyfriends or girlfriends. While these are not bad things, they are not where God would have us place our confidence, and they will undoubtedly fail us at times. He sent His Son to forgive us, grant us new life, and support us while we wait for His final coming in glory.

CLOSING (5 minutes)

Invite the students to think about false promises they may rely on instead of God. Let them pray individually, in pairs, or as a group using this model: "Dear God, please help ("me" or name of student) trust more in You this week. Thank You for Your strength in Christ. Amen."

LESSON EXTENDER

✝ Invite the students to reflect on things they expect to happen within the next one, three, and ten years—personal goals (graduating from college), global events (peace in the Mideast), or technological advances (high school education through the Internet). How might these things demonstrate God's power?

✝ What promises are Christians today looking forward to seeing fulfilled? Besides the time we will be with Jesus in heaven, to what other things can we look forward?

The Real Deal

WHICH ONE IS REAL?
Check which definition you think is the right one for the word above it:

gramarye
- __ **a.** Having to do with the proper use of language
- __ **b.** Having to do with magic or the occult
- __ **c.** Having to do with weights and measures
- __ **d.** A type of grain

pash
- __ **a.** To smash something
- __ **b.** Eccentric, ritzy
- __ **c.** An ornamental window decoration
- __ **d.** An off-white color

sporran
- __ **a.** Old, weathered condition
- __ **b.** A type of pouch, or purse
- __ **c.** A medieval lance or spear
- __ **d.** The spoke of a spinning wheel

PROMISES, PROMISES

What is the most outrageous claim or promise you can remember seeing in a newspaper, magazine, billboard, or television advertisement?

....

Why do you think people fall for these claims or promises?

....

When was a time you were "taken" by some sort of claim or promise?

....

Read **Matthew 11:1–5**.

1. What were John's disciples looking for? (especially **verses 2–3**)

....
....

2. What "proof" did Jesus give to tell them He was the one? **(verse 5)**

....
....

Read **Mark 2:1–12**.

3. What proof did Jesus give to show He had the authority to forgive sins? **(verses 10–11)**

....
....

4. What else did this prove about Jesus? **(verse 7)**

....
....

CHOOSE WHAT'S REAL

Jesus was the "real thing," showing up the false promises and claims of the world and humankind for what they were. He proved the truth of the Gospel by forgiving sins and providing physical healing.

....
....
....
....
....

What are some false promises you or others might be leaning on that compete with Jesus?

....
....
....
....

STUDENT PAGE 19

Journey of Faith © 2007 Concordia Publishing House. Reproduced by permission.

28. IN MOMENTS OF NEED

Mark 5:25–34

Lesson Focus

Jesus is never too busy for us. He loves each of His children and cares for us in our greatest moments of need.

OPENING (15 minutes)

Ask students, "If you could have God change something about you, what would you want Him to change? How would this change affect you? Would it be private or noticed by other people? How would it change your attitude about yourself?"

THE INSIDE STORY (15 minutes)

Distribute copies of the student page. Have the students open their Bibles to Mark 5:21–43. Read verses 25–34 aloud, but scan the other verses as well. Ask students to recall the story before and after verses 25–34. Many of us know the story about Jairus's daughter, but this story of the bleeding woman happens right in the middle of the other story. As you review the other questions in this section, remind students that, even when Jesus was focused on the task ahead (dealing with Jairus's daughter), He was able to meet the needs of this woman. He has time to deal with all our needs. Note that the girl was twelve—the woman bled for twelve years. Jesus called them both "daughter." Most important—He touched them. Because He was God in human form, He could touch them. It was a sign of the incarnation—God becoming man. This is important because Christ had to be true man in order to pay the penalty of man's sin. He had to be true God to be able to take on the sin of the whole world victoriously and rise from the dead.

GET INSIDE THE STORY (15 minutes)

Divide students into breakout groups, allowing them time to review the questions in this section. When groups have completed their work, discuss their findings as a whole group.

The woman in the story was in need but didn't want to bother Jesus. Perhaps she thought that Jesus was more concerned about the synagogue ruler and his problem. After all, Jairus was somebody important. But Jesus refused to stop looking for her until He found her.

What's the good news? Jesus cared as much for the woman as the synagogue ruler's daughter. Because of her ongoing condition, Jewish society considered this woman to be very dirty; no one would have touched her or helped her. Jesus showed no favoritism between the woman and Jairus but took the time to give the woman what she really needed. More than just physical healing, she needed the healing that can only come from the peace of Jesus Christ. Jesus made her just as important as the other person and healed both people in their time of need.

What does this tell you about how Jesus deals with our problems? He doesn't always work on our timetable, but we know He gives us what we need and that He loves all of His children equally. We know this because He has already dealt with our ultimate problem—sin and death.

CLOSING (5 minutes)

Dear Jesus, thank You for always taking the time to hear us and give us what we really need. We know that You give us hope when no one else can. In Your name we pray. Amen.

IN MOMENTS OF NEED

THE INSIDE STORY
What is the story in **Mark 5:21–43**?

....

What is the story in **Mark 5:25–34**?

....

What special point do you think the Gospel writer was trying to make by putting one story in the middle of another?

....

....

What similarities or parallels do you see with these two stories?

....

....

GET INSIDE THE STORY
How do you think the woman felt after suffering for twelve years and spending all her money, only to get worse instead of better?

....

....

What did Jesus offer her that doctors couldn't?

....

Why do you think the woman didn't want to bother Jesus?

....

....

Why do you think the disciples were urging Jesus to keep heading toward Jairus's house instead of searching for the woman?

....

....

When the woman confessed that she had touched Jesus, do you think she was worried about being in trouble?

....

Journey of Faith © 2007 Concordia Publishing House. Reproduced by permission.

STUDENT PAGE 20

21. WHY TRUST?

Mark 1:29–39

Lesson Focus

In Scripture, Jesus tells His followers that He has come to proclaim the Good News that the kingdom of God is near. Through this lesson, students will understand how Jesus' death and resurrection makes the kingdom a reality in their lives today.

OPENING (5 minutes)

Tell the class you want to blindfold someone and do something to this person, but you won't tell him or her what. Ask for a volunteer, then blindfold him and ask him to stick out his hand. Put a piece of candy, money, or some kind of prize in it. Explain that this little object lesson is a lot like faith in God. Jesus came that we might learn to trust in Him and thereby receive the incredible gift of new life He offers us. But just as some of your students were hesitant to trust and put on the blindfold, many people in the world today are hesitant to trust in Jesus. Introduce the next section by saying something like, "In today's lesson, we want to see how God works great faith, not only in our hearts, but in those of unbelievers as well."

EXAMINING THE EVIDENCE (15 minutes)

Distribute copies of the student page to your class. Read the directions printed on the page, and direct students to complete the activity either individually or in pairs. After ten minutes or so, ask them to share what they discovered. After your students have shared their observations, explain that the healing and casting out of demons were a part of Jesus' "proclaiming" the Gospel. They did not create faith in Jesus as the Messiah, but demonstrated to those who came to faith that He was the promised Messiah. The Old Testament Scriptures (Psalm 103:3; Isaiah 61:1–3; Malachi 4:2) pointed to a Messiah who would do the things Jesus was doing. Mark 1:29–39 tells of the signs accompanying His words that the kingdom of God was at hand. Many people experienced Jesus' works, heard His Word, and trusted in Him.

TRUSTING HIM (15 minutes)

Use the questions found on the student page for discussion as a whole group.

Use the discussion to remind your students that God has given us the sign of the cross, the indisputable testimony of His love for us through Jesus' death and resurrection. He tells us that through His Spirit people are enabled to believe (John 6:35–40; 10:27–28) and through His Word their faith and trust in Him grows (Romans 1:16; 10:17).

CLOSING (7 minutes)

Read **Psalm 121** together as a benediction. Take time to have students pray for greater trust and that God might use them to encourage others to trust in Jesus.

LESSON EXTENDER

✞ Have students read Psalm 19 and list the good things God's Word does for them.

WHY TRUST?

EXAMINING THE EVIDENCE

As soon as they left the synagogue, they went with James and John to the home of Simon and Andrew. Simon's mother-in-law was in bed with a fever, and they told Jesus about her. So He went to her, took her hand and helped her up. The fever left her and she began to wait on them. That evening after sunset the people brought to Jesus all the sick and demon-possessed. The whole town gathered at the door, and Jesus healed many who had various diseases. He also drove out many demons, but He would not let the demons speak because they knew who He was. Very early in the morning, while it was still dark, Jesus got up, left the house and went off to a solitary place, where He prayed. Simon and his companions went to look for Him, and when they found Him, they exclaimed: "Everyone is looking for You!" Jesus replied, "Let us go somewhere else—to the nearby villages—so I can preach there also. That is why I have come." So He traveled throughout Galilee, preaching in their synagogues and driving out demons. **Mark 1:29–39**

Read the passage above; then do the following:
Underline the miracles

⬅ Draw an arrow from the word Jesus that points to whomever He helped.

Ⓒircle the reason Jesus said He had come.

★ Put a star by anything you think is important in this passage.

How do **Psalm 103:3** and **Isaiah 61:1–3** give evidence of Christ as the Messiah?

TRUSTING HIM

Many people have a difficult time trusting Jesus today. Why do you think that is?

If they were present at the home of Peter's mother-in-law and saw what the disciples saw, do you think people would trust in Jesus? Why or why not?

What do people need to "see" in order to trust in Jesus? (I pray that God would open the eyes of your faith . . .)

Why doesn't God do spectacular miracles to get people to trust today?

How do people who won't see Jesus physically know He is the Savior? (See **John 20:29–31**.)

Journey of Faith © 2007 Concordia Publishing House. Reproduced by permission.

STUDENT PAGE 21

22. WHY DID THIS HAPPEN?

John 9

Lesson Focus

Jesus' death and resurrection provide proof that God has a purpose, working for our good and His glory, even through difficult and tragic situations in our lives.

JONI'S STORY (15 minutes)

Collect a variety of newspaper and magazine articles that highlight human tragedies. Distribute one story to each group of three or four students and have them discuss why they think this tragedy occurred. Ask your students to share personal stories of tragedy or affliction that were difficult to understand.

Distribute copies of the student page to each person. Ask someone to read "Joni's Story." Lead a discussion of the questions posed at the end of the story.

GOD HAS A PURPOSE (20 minutes)

The disciples witnessed a similar situation in John 9. Ask student volunteers to read the passages out loud. Use the questions on the student page to help your class think about what they just read. The disciples assumed that sin led to this man's blindness as a punishment. Jesus points out that some tragedies occur for other reasons, all in relation to God's will that all people become saved (1 Timothy 2:3). Sometimes tragedy affects just the one who suffers. Other times God touches others as well. Sometimes God's glory is evident to many.

Ask the class how God's work might be seen in the life of Joni. What good might God bring through her situation? Allow them to voice their thoughts, then explain that God used Joni's tragedy to draw her closer to Himself. Through her recovery and learning to adapt to her paralysis, Jesus' death and resurrection became the very real power behind her reason for living. She now heads up an international ministry to disabled people, helping them find hope and wholeness through a personal relationship with Jesus Christ.

Jesus' death and resurrection prove that God is present in our struggles and is working for His glory and our good. God, in love, gave His Son to die for us. That same love is at work in our lives. Ask your students to write Romans 8:28 in the space provided on the student page.

SEEING GOD'S PURPOSE (15 minutes)

Direct students to the student page. Ask them to think about how God might work in each of the situations listed. After discussing the first two, ask students to think of a tough situation they or someone close to them is facing. Have them write it in the space provided. Discuss how God might use that situation to bring the person closer to Jesus and to show His glory to others.

PRAYER (5 minutes)

Close your time together by having group members pray about the situations they wrote down.

LESSON EXTENDER

✝ Challenge students to memorize Romans 8:28 by writing it on a card and sticking it on their bedroom wall or bathroom mirror.

✝ Encourage students to pray for those who are struggling and share with them the good news that God is with them in their struggle. How might they help others know God's presence? Sharing a Bible story or Scripture verse, or sending notes with a prayer are all good possibilities.

WHY DID THIS HAPPEN?

JONI'S STORY
Joni seemed to have it made. A popular Christian teenager, she was pretty much guaranteed a college athletic scholarship and life was looking good. That is—until one fateful dive into a lake during summer vacation. The result: a broken neck, which left her paralyzed from her shoulders down for the rest of her life. As she lay in the hospital bed, she wanted to die. Her life as she knew it was gone and all she could think of was how cruel God must be.

Do you think God "did" this to her? Why or why not?

If God allowed it, could He also have prevented it?

If you were Joni, what would you be thinking about God?

GOD HAS A PURPOSE
Read **John 9.**

What was the assumption of the disciples in **verse 2**?

What assumptions do people sometimes make about God when bad things happen? For instance, if a child gets hit by a car and is killed, what do people say about God's involvement?

What was Jesus' response in **verse 3** to their question?

How was the work of God displayed in this man's life?

Look at **verses 8–11, 16–17, 30–33, 35–38**.

After reading this story, why do you think God allowed the man to be born blind?

Who was really "blind" at the end of the story? Blind to what?

Write out **Romans 8:28.** How did this apply to the man born blind? to you?

SEEING GOD'S PURPOSE
Tom had been really looking forward to the camping trip next weekend. But after breaking his ankle, he's going to be stuck at home with his parents and grandma. All he can think of is the great time he'll be missing.

Sarah had all the skills to really succeed as an actress and singer. But with the onset of juvenile diabetes, it looks like her dreams are crushed. She's wondering why God would take away her whole purpose for living.

Your/your friend's situation:

Journey of Faith © 2007 Concordia Publishing House. Reproduced by permission.

STUDENT PAGE 22

23. Even the Wind and the Waves

Matthew 8:23–27

Lesson Focus

Jesus is with us, no matter how great the troubles. No obstacle is insurmountable for Jesus.

WHO'S AFRAID? (5 minutes)

Spiders, mice, snakes, the dark, small places—everyone is afraid of something. What scares you? Fear is the most basic of emotions. It sparks our fight or flight instinct. Have everyone, including yourself, share his or her fears, real or imagined. Guide the sharing so that no feelings are hurt. The more you share, the more it will be okay for students to share.

LORD, SAVE US! (5 minutes)

The disciples know that Jesus has the power to save them, and yet they are still afraid. This is true for us today. Our hearts recognize what Jesus can do, but our heads tell us to be afraid. How does our fear affect our prayer life? How do we respond to Jesus when He answers us?

YOU OF LITTLE FAITH (20 minutes)

Break into pairs or groups and research the biblical people whom Matthew holds up as examples of having great faith. How can this "great cloud of witnesses" serve as a reminder to us when we are afraid?

EVEN THE WIND AND THE WAVES (15 minutes)

Students of all ages always find it astonishing that the disciples witnessed the awesome power of God in Jesus and still managed to say, "Who is this . . . ?" Yet we, too, are amazed by what Christ can do. Use the passages in this section to discuss how Christ's divinity and power reassure us.

CLOSING (5 minutes)

Read Psalm 146 responsively as your closing prayer. Sing "I Will Call upon the Lord" (*Singing Saints* 16) or "Eternal Father, Strong to Save" (*Hymnal Supplement 98* 906).

LESSON EXTENDER

✝ Discuss other "impossible" situations where nothing is impossible for God.
   David and Goliath
   Daniel in the lions' den
   Shadrach, Meshach, and Abednego
   Jesus' birth
   The resurrection of Lazarus

Even the Wind and the Waves

LORD, SAVE US!
Read **Matthew 8:23–27**. What do the disciples want from Jesus?

....

How do they react when they get what they want?

....

What do you want from Jesus?

....

How do you react to His answer to your prayer?

....

YOU OF LITTLE FAITH
In addition to this story, Matthew records three other instances where Jesus criticized the disciples for their "little faith" **(Matthew 6:30; 14:31; 16:8)**. By contrast, the evangelist records six examples of great faith. Who demonstrated their faith in these passages? How can they be an example for us?

Matthew 8:2

....

Matthew 8:10

....

Matthew 9:18

....

Matthew 9:28

....

Matthew 14:36

....

Matthew 15:28

....

EVEN THE WIND AND THE WAVES
In the calming of the storm, we see both Christ's humanity in His exhaustion and Christ's deity in His rebuke. What reassurances do these passages give us that, even in times of trouble, the wind and the waves obey Him?

Psalm 89:9

....

Isaiah 41:13

....

Isaiah 51:15

....

John 16:33

....

Journey of Faith © 2007 Concordia Publishing House. Reproduced by permission.

24. CLEANING HOUSE

John 2:13–22

Lesson Focus

Jesus is the new temple, and the fullness of God resides in Him. He clears away all things that take the focus off of God.

OPENING (5 minutes)

Before the study begins, clutter up the meeting space, especially the area near the front of the class, with as many distractions as you can. Include items that students might want to play with such as handheld games. To begin, ask the students if they feel that this is the best environment to focus on the Bible. Why? Transition by saying that there are distractions in the Church and our lives that can take the focus off of Christ, but He can help us clear them away.

TEMPLE TRASH (15 minutes)

Read together John 2:13–22. Have students work in breakout groups to answer the questions. Discuss their findings, noting the following possible answers:

People were required to give only temple coins and offer only clean sacrifices. The money changers and merchants were making excess profits, which was like stealing from the common people. They were taking the focus off of God. Jesus shows anger, but even His response was not sinful. Righteous anger may be in defense of the things of God and is opposed to sin. Righteous anger does not act out of sinful motivation. The people had lost their way and their focus on God. The temple was not God's sacred space anymore. Jesus was both the sacrifice and the Most Holy Place. Jesus was far superior to the building.

PERSONAL CLEANING (15 minutes)

Discuss the questions from this section as a whole group, noting the following: Answers will vary, but may include programs; arguments over worship style; non-biblical traditions; or any unnecessary, idolatrous, or distracting thing. Distractions will vary, but may include video games, telephone calls, movies, television, or the Internet. People will respond in faith or in unbelief. How might they show a response of unbelief?

WASHED CLEAN (15 minutes)

Conclude this lesson by discussing the implication of Baptism. Discuss the questions from the student page as a whole group. (Note: In John 3, Jesus tells Nicodemus how to be reborn and become clean.) In Baptism we died with Christ and are given new life and forgiveness of sins (Romans 6:4; Colossians 2:12). The washing of Baptism cleanses and cleans out the clutter of sin in our lives. We can go directly to God in prayer through Jesus. God is everywhere, not located in one place, and we can talk to Him from anywhere. Close with a group prayer.

LESSON EXTENDER

Discuss with the students the implications of the splitting of the temple curtain recorded in both Matthew 27:51 and Mark 15:38. How does this event relate to today's lesson?

Cleaning House

TEMPLE TRASH
Read together **John 2:13–22**.

The money changers and merchants were necessary for people to buy acceptable sacrifices and give the proper temple coins. Why do you think Jesus saw a problem with what was going on?

Describe Jesus' actions and attitude at the temple. Why might He have felt that way?

When is it not a sin to be angry?

What do you think was at the heart of Jesus' anger?

Compare Jesus, the new temple, with the temple in Jerusalem.

PERSONAL CLEANING
What things might Jesus want to clean out of the Church today? Why?

What would Jesus come to clear out of your life that can take the focus away from God?

Identify different ways to respond to Jesus' cleaning up your life.

WASHED CLEAN
Jesus clears out the clutter from the temple in today's passage. How could this imagery compare to Baptism? (See **Romans 6:4**; **Colossians 2:12**.)

What does it mean that Jesus is the temple?

What is most exciting about Jesus' cleansing your life?

Journey of Faith © 2007 Concordia Publishing House. Reproduced by permission.

STUDENT PAGE 24

25. MEASURING UP

Mark 2:18–22; Galatians 5:19–25

Lesson Focus

Teenagers feel lots of pressure to live up to other people's expectations. God measures us not by what we do, but by who we are—His precious children and disciples.

OPENING (10 minutes)

Describe or display two sets of clothes: one dirty, wrinkled, torn, and stained; the other new, clean, and pressed. Ask the students which clothes they would put on after showering before a party? Ask when they might put on the old, dirty set of clothes. (They might say, "When I want to be comfortable" or "If I know I'm going to get dirty again." Remember these responses for later.)

Point out that the clothes are symbols of our spiritual life. Our sinful nature makes us dirty with sin. However, we are washed clean and made new through the blood of Jesus.

INSPECTION (5 minutes)

Distribute copies of the student page. Point out that clothes are one way people judge others. Invite the students to suggest other ways. Discuss the expectations of parents, teachers, coaches, and others. Ask, "What is the toughest expectation you feel?"

EVALUATION (20 minutes)

Read Mark 2:18–22. Point out that people expected Jesus and His disciples to observe certain religious activities, including fasting. Look up the Bible passages about fasting. People fasted in Old Testament times as a sign of (1) repentance (1 Samuel 7:6); (2) humility (Ezra 8:21); and (3) mourning for sin (Joel 2:12). In Acts 13:2–3, fasting accompanies prayer. Fasting is an external sign of the Spirit's internal work. It can be a useful spiritual tool, but it is not a means of manipulating God, who already loves us, knows our hearts, and acts according to His grace.

In Mark 2:19, Jesus shows us when fasting is not the best response. He has forgiven us. He is with us now and forever. We should celebrate, not mourn or fast.

RENEWAL (15 minutes)

Remind the students of the reasons they might put on old, dirty clothes (to be "comfortable" or because they "know they are going to get dirty again"). Satan tempts us to sin in similar ways. Sometimes he pulls us back to the sinful, comfortable way of doing things. At other times, we give up doing right because we're "going to sin again anyway." Read the Galatians passages and discuss the questions below the boxes. (1) Through the waters of Baptism, the Holy Spirit gives faith and complete forgiveness for sin. The Spirit provides the seed and nourishment for the fruits of the Spirit growing in us. (2) Keeping in step with the Spirit results from God's work in us through His Word. The motive comes from Him; the specifics may include all aspects of the Christian life—worship, daily devotions, and acts of service. Challenge the students to list some specific intentions for their week.

CLOSING (5 minutes)

Close with a prayer thanking Jesus for His free gift of life and love. Ask Him for the strength to "keep in step with the Spirit" and live in joy and gratitude.

LESSON EXTENDER

✝ Remind your students of Jesus' words in Matthew 5:17. There is nothing we can do to earn God's favor. In our sinful nature, we don't want to. Through Christ's fulfillment of the Law, we are made new and empowered to both desire and do God's will.

Measuring Up

THE BEST!

INSPECTION
What are some ways that young people are judged by adults or other youth?

....

....

....

....

EVALUATION
Read **Mark 2:18–22**. For what are Jesus' disciples being criticized?

....

....

What reasons does the Bible give for fasting?
1 Samuel 7:6

....

....

Ezra 8:21

....

....

Joel 2:12

....

....

Acts 13:2–3

....

....

What reason does Jesus give for *not* fasting? **Mark 2:19**

....

....

....

RENEWAL
Galatians 5:19–21 lists attitudes and actions from which we, as Christians, should fast, things we should give up. Choose those you struggle with the most and write them in the "old" box below.

Read **Galatians 5:22–25**. These are the fruits of our new life in Christ. We never need to fast from these. Choose the ones you demonstrate the most and write them in the "new" box.

Old	New

Where does this spiritual fruit come from?

....

....

How can you "keep in step with the Spirit" this week?

....

....

....

STUDENT PAGE 25

Journey of Faith © 2007 Concordia Publishing House. Reproduced by permission.

26. NEWBORN

John 3:1–21

Lesson Focus
We can be confident in God's love for us demonstrated in Christ's sacrifice for sin.

OPENING (10 minutes)

If you can arrange it beforehand, have students and adult leaders bring in their baby pictures. Plan an activity around it—guess whose picture is whose, or vote for the cutest baby, biggest baby, and baldest baby. Give away prizes. As an option, bring in photos of babies from magazines and have students vote on those photos.

THE BASICS (15 minutes)

Distribute copies of the student page, and read together John 3:1–21. Divide students into breakout groups to answer the questions from the student page. Review their answers.

Nicodemus was a Pharisee, a member of the Jewish ruling council, and a teacher. Nicodemus chose to approach Jesus at night. He may have feared the reaction of his fellow Pharisees if he had been seen with Jesus. He may also have avoided the daytime crowds surrounding Jesus so he could get Jesus' undivided attention. Jesus explains that He (the Son of Man) must be lifted up, referring to His crucifixion. The cross was the supreme exaltation of Jesus. Like the children of Israel who were saved from death by looking at the bronze serpent that Moses raised in the desert, so those who believe in Christ as Lord and Savior will not see eternal death.

Some possibilities to discuss include verse 3, born again; verse 15, Moses lifting up the snake in the desert; verse 17, God did not send His Son to condemn the world; and verse 18, whoever believes in Jesus is not condemned.

UP CLOSE AND PERSONAL (10 minutes)

Invite students to complete this section of the student page. Encourage students to share their answers with the whole group. Help students to see that the things they value more highly may involve greater sacrifice.

THE JOY AND THE PAIN (15 minutes)

Read together Romans 8:18–25. Discuss how giving birth is one of the most painful but also most joyful experiences in the world. (Perhaps you could even invite a mother of a newborn to share her experience.) Salvation can be painful if we cling to things of the world or suffer for the sake of Jesus' cause. Salvation is joyful through faith in Christ.

It's painful to leave our old life and habits behind. Sometimes our heart breaks over it. God's heart breaks at the sinful condition of the world. Salvation is joyful because it's a new life of forgiveness, bringing security in Christ and excitement about living out God's will in our lives with the help of His Spirit. In John 3:15, Jesus talks about how His life must be sacrificed for the salvation of the world.

Have students answer the questions about sacrifice on the student page, then help them understand the ultimate sacrifice: although Jesus challenges us to make sacrifices so that we can grow spiritually, He made the greatest sacrifice, which we couldn't make—paying for our own sins. He gives us power through the Holy Spirit willingly to sacrifice our own desires as we strive to do His will.

CLOSING (5 minutes)

Close with a prayer, thanking God for the sacrifice of His Son for us as His children. Be sure to include any specific prayer requests that the students may have.

Newborn

THE BASICS
Read **John 3:1–21**.

Who was Nicodemus?

Why might it have been an advantage to approach Jesus at night?

What did Jesus say must happen for someone to have eternal life in **verses 14–15**? What does He mean?

John 3:16 is probably the best-known verse in the entire Bible. If you could use one phrase in this passage to share the Gospel, besides **John 3:16**, what phrase or idea would it be and why?

UP CLOSE AND PERSONAL
What do you have to sacrifice

to get a good grade on a final?

for a quality friendship?

to make a sports team?

to grow as a Christian?

What would be hard for you to give up in any of these circumstances?

THE JOY AND THE PAIN
Read **Romans 8:18–25**.

How can our salvation be both painful and joyful?

What did God choose to give up for our salvation?

What sacrifices do you think God might be asking you to make this week as a response to His sacrifice for you on the cross?

STUDENT PAGE 26

Journey of Faith © 2007 Concordia Publishing House. Reproduced by permission.

27. Living Water

John 4:1–42

Lesson Focus

Jesus is the only source of refreshment for our souls; He can satisfy our dying thirst.

RUNNING ON EMPTY
(10 minutes)

Have a short discussion on everyone's favorite drink. What will quench their thirst when they are really parched, and what won't? Physically, we are often running on empty—not enough sleep or exercise, skipping breakfast, not enough nutritious food. How do our bodies react when we run out of energy? We can run out of energy spiritually too. What causes our reservoirs to be depleted? How can we refuel?

WATER, WATER, EVERYWHERE
(25 minutes)

The analogy of Jesus as living water is a powerful one. Key features of this story to share are the importance of Jesus approaching a Samaritan woman (John 4:1–8), the one-on-one discussion between the two (verses 9–26), the recognition by the woman of Jesus as a prophet (verses 19–20), and the salvation that came to the woman and others of her village that day (verses 39–42).

From there, lead into what Jesus offers us today. The Samaritans in the town believed when they heard Jesus for themselves. We are led to faith by the Spirit through Baptism and the Word of God. Baptism is another source of the same living water that Jesus offered the woman to drink. It waters our sin-parched souls with eternal life. Look at Revelation 21:1–6. Christ is the living water. In Him we have forgiveness, life, and salvation. He is the Word of God (John 1:1).

NOT A DROP TO DRINK
(15 minutes)

Using the references, discuss how Jesus' living water satisfies our dying thirst. Through His death and resurrection, Christ has fulfilled the Law and satisfies our thirst for life and salvation. Through the Spirit, Christ freely invites all to receive the gift of eternal life.

CLOSING (5 minutes)

Pray Psalm 23 together. Sing "Come, Thou Fount of Every Blessing" (*LSB* 686; *HS98* 876).

LESSON EXTENDER

✝ Continue the analogy of Christ being food for our souls with a discussion of the institution of the Lord's Supper from Luke 22 and 1 Corinthians 10 and 11.

✝ How does Christ's very body and blood, in, with, and under the bread and wine, satisfy our spiritual hunger? How does Jesus' description of Himself as the bread of life in John 6 add to this analogy?

Living Water

RUNNING ON EMPTY
Our physical bodies are often running on empty. In what ways does our body let us know it needs to be refueled?

....

....

Our spiritual body also needs to be refueled often. How do we know?

....

....

What are the signs when we are spiritually dragging?

....

....

....

WATER, WATER, EVERYWHERE
Read about Jesus' one-on-one conversation with the Samaritan woman at Jacob's well in **John 4:1–42**.

Why was the Samaritan woman surprised when Jesus spoke to her?

....

What does this tell you about Jesus' compassion?

....

What was the woman looking for?

....

What did Jesus offer her?

....

What does Jesus offer us? How do you know?

....

NOT A DROP TO DRINK
Read **John 7:37–38; Revelation 7:17; 21:1–6;** and **22:17**. How does Jesus' living water satisfy our dying thirst?

....

....

STUDENT PAGE 27

Journey of Faith © 2007 Concordia Publishing House. Reproduced by permission.

28. Father Loves Best

Luke 15:1–3, 11–32

Lesson Focus

Despite our willful sin, God, our gracious Father, welcomes His repentant children back with open arms!

I'M OUT OF HERE! (10 minutes)

Have students respond to the statement. They are beginning to look forward to the perceived freedoms of adulthood and living on their own. Encourage their discussion and comments.

UNGRATEFUL SON NUMBER ONE (10 minutes)

Complete this section as a whole group. The younger son apparently wants his father to give him his "share" of the inheritance (which was not the normal thing to do). His intention to spend the money as he pleases, free from his father's controls, becomes evident. His attitude seems pretty arrogant and rude. He doesn't even *ask* his father for what he wants. His request is more of a demand. Verse 17 says, "When he came to his senses," indicating a lack of sense in his former state. It would be easy to focus on the younger son, his "wild living," and what a rotten son he had been. That would miss the main point, though. *The most important character in this story is the father.*

FORGIVING FATHER (15 minutes)

Allow students to work in breakout groups. When groups have finished working, discuss as a whole group. Thinking about potential parental responses could prompt some interesting discussion. Try to focus a little more on how students might respond if they were in the parent role. It may be necessary to point out that the son took, and lost, quite a considerable amount of money. He also acted in rebellious opposition to the ways in which he had been instructed at home. The things the father actually did could be similar to the following: The father welcomed his son back with open arms and great celebration as a treasured member of the family. He put the best robe on his son, a ring on his finger, and sandals on his feet. The father killed the fattened calf and had a feast prepared in celebration of his son's return. His actions indicate the unfathomable bounds of his love, mercy, and grace toward his son.

UNGRATEFUL SON NUMBER TWO (10 minutes)

The older son is resentful with a self-righteous jealousy that the disobedient younger son would be treated so well. Some may argue that the older son is justified in his anger. After all, he did not disobey in the same very blatant way. He also, however, did not share in the father's joy at the return and repentance of his brother. He takes on an extremely self-righteous attitude and pouts instead. Valid discussion for this point may vary considerably. The discussion of being more like the younger or older son may make some on both sides uncomfortable or even defensive. Chances are that among a group of students choosing to attend Bible study, there may be more "older sons." Encourage discussion, but you may also wish to ask questions about how "bad kids" are treated when they come to church or even just try to associate with "good kids." Don't let students off the hook too easily in either direction.

WHO ARE THESE CHARACTERS? (5 minutes)

The younger son represents repentant sinners. The Father represents our gracious God. The older son represents the Pharisees (those who do good and tend to stand in judgment over others). Depending on the direction of discussion throughout the lesson, you may wish to emphasize that the point is not that "being good" is bad. Keep the wrap-up focused on the gracious love and mercy of our heavenly Father toward us as His sons and daughters. Remind students what forgiveness this means for their repentant hearts, even if what they have done feels unforgivable.

Close in prayer, thanking God for His unfathomable grace, mercy, and forgiveness. Ask God to work His love in our hearts that we may be better able to extend that same kind of forgiveness and love to others.

Father Loves Best

I'M OUT OF HERE!
What about moving out of your parents' home and being on your own most appeals to you?

_____ Being able to make my own rules

_____ Being able to make my own decisions and set my own priorities

_____ Having the responsibility to support myself and be self-sufficient

_____ I'm not looking forward to leaving. I want to live at home forever.

Read **Luke 15:1–3, 11–32**.

UNGRATEFUL SON NUMBER ONE
What does the younger son want from his father? Why do you think he wants this? **(verses 12–13)**

How would you describe his attitude?

How does **verse 17** reflect on what his state of mind had been during his "adventure"?

FORGIVING FATHER
How do you think your parents would react if you had done what the younger son did and then dragged yourself back home?

How do you think you would respond if you were the parent of the son?

After each statement about what the younger son was hoping the father would do, write what the father actually did.

"Maybe Dad will let me have a job as a servant."

"Maybe Dad will let me have some clothes."

"Maybe Dad will let me have some food."

What do the father's actions reflect about his character?

UNGRATEFUL SON NUMBER TWO
Let's take a brief look at the older son—the good son, the son who never disobeyed his father (at least according to him).

Why was the older son so upset?

Do you believe he is "justified" in his anger? Why or why not?

Are you more like the younger son or the older son in your actions and attitudes?

WHO ARE THESE CHARACTERS?
Match the characters of the story with those they represent.

_____ The younger son

_____ The father

_____ The older son

A. The Pharisees (those who do good and tend to stand in judgment over others)

B. Repentant sinners

C. Our gracious and forgiving God

STUDENT PAGE 28

Journey of Faith © 2007 Concordia Publishing House. Reproduced by permission.

29. WHO'S MY NEIGHBOR?

Luke 10:25–37;
Micah 6:8;
Matthew 5:7;
Luke 6:36

Lesson Focus

The word *neighbors* implies those who live nearby. Jesus has another definition. In this study, students will be led to discover a broader definition of *neighbors*—those who are touched by and touch others with God's mercy.

OPENING (10 minutes)

Ask your class, "Does anyone here have $5.00? I need a little extra for lunch after church." If they ask, tell them you are not planning on paying them back. Ask, "If someone you did not know came up to you and asked for a handout, what would you do?" Ask those to whom this has really happened to share their experiences.

THE ISSUE (10 minutes)

Distribute copies of the student page. Have a student read the quotation. Point out that many may feel this way. Ask, "Why do you think that they would make this statement? How would you respond?"

THE WORD (20 minutes)

Group students in fours. Have each person in the group look up one of the Bible passages in this section. Then have them share answers within the group.

After they are done, ask, "What concept is common to all these passages?" (Mercy or some form of it.) Ask for a definition of mercy. According to the dictionary, mercy is being kind and compassionate in your treatment of another person. Have the students take turns reading Luke 10:25–37 verse by verse and discuss the questions on the student page. Make sure students realize that our "neighborly" ways are possible only because Jesus is our "neighbor." He showed mercy for us by dying for our sins and working in us through the Spirit to give us new life.

THE WORLD (15 minutes)

Have the students read the situation on the student page to themselves. Ask, "What kind of problem could come up at three in the morning?" Let volunteers share responses to the question "Whom would you call?" Point out that God loves them and will provide help in direct and indirect ways—through events and through caring people.

Ask the students to think about someone in their school, neighborhood, or family who needs help in some way right now—a person they could assist this week. Allow students time to think through and write down some ways they could help.

CLOSING (5 minutes)

Close with a prayer that God would help the students reach out in mercy to the people who need help and that He would encourage them to do so daily.

LESSON EXTENDER

✝ Have the students commit to reporting about the person they needed to show mercy to and how they felt.

✝ Plan a class outing to extend a hand of mercy to someone in your community.

WHO'S MY NEIGHBOR?

THE ISSUE
"Religious people are supposed to act a certain way, right? I mean, they're supposed to help the poor, get involved with community events, help their neighbors, and stuff. If I can't expect help from a person who goes to church, whom can I expect it from?" Do you agree? How would you respond?

....
....

THE WORD
Review these four passages. Look for God's plan for you.

Luke 10:36–37; Micah 6:8; Matthew 5:7; Luke 6:36

How is the message in each of these passages consistent?

....
....
....
....
....

Read **Luke 10:25–37**.

What is God calling His people to do?

....
....

How is that possible?

....
....

THE WORLD
It's 3:00 a.m. and you have a problem . . . a big one. Whom could you call? It would have to be someone you could trust, who would be there for you with both their head and their heart.

Whom would you call? Why?

....
....
....

Whom do you know right now who is hurting and may have no one to call on for assistance? Can you be the merciful one in that person's life?

....
....
....

Take time to develop a simple plan to make yourself available to this person to share God's mercy in helpful ways.

....
....
....
....
....

Journey of Faith © 2007 Concordia Publishing House. Reproduced by permission.

STUDENT PAGE 29

34. LORD, IF YOU HAD BEEN THERE . . .

John 11:1–46

Lesson Focus

Most believers can point to a time or experience when it seemed as if God just wasn't there. God promises that He will not leave or forsake His people. His Son, Jesus, was present for Mary and Martha, was present on the cross for us, and is present in our lives through the power of the Spirit.

OPENING (10 minutes)

Millions of people rely on 911 as the number to dial for emergencies. Ask the class to imagine that for one day the 911 system is out of service. What might happen during that day? In a crisis, people rely on more powerful or able people to rescue them.

OUT TO LUNCH (10 minutes)

Is God always there? Distribute copies of the student page and direct the students to fill in their answers for this section. Let volunteers share their examples.

TAKING GOD SERIOUSLY (20 minutes)

We are not the first people to feel as if God has overlooked them. Jesus' closest friends knew He was the Son of God, but they still felt He wasn't there for them. Ask volunteers to read aloud John 11:1–45. Consider reading it like a play.

Discuss the questions on the student page. Remind the students that Jesus was not ignoring His friends' plight. Jesus planned to do much more than heal a sick friend—He planned to demonstrate God's power and point people to God's kingdom.

HERE TODAY—HERE TOMORROW! (10 minutes)

There's an old saying: "Here today, gone tomorrow." Jesus is not a fair-weather friend. What is really happening when we, like Martha and Mary, think God is ignoring our crisis? Let students answer. Direct the students to read Acts 18:9–10 and answer the questions on the student page. Let volunteers share their insights.

CLOSING (5 minutes)

Direct the class to read aloud Acts 17:26–27 from the student page. These words remind us of God's care for His people throughout time. Lead the class in a prayer of thanksgiving for the special people named by class members as special agents of God.

LESSON EXTENDER

✝ Suggest that students study Jesus' prayer in John 11:41–42. Challenge students to write a prayer like His, containing confidence, purpose, and thanksgiving.

✝ Ask students to choose one of the events they listed in the "Out to Lunch" section and reconsider how God was involved in the event. Think of ways in which He may have been showing His love.

LORD, IF YOU HAD BEEN THERE . . .

OUT TO LUNCH
Are there events or situations that make you think God is "out to lunch" and not watching what's going on in the world? Give an example.

....
....
....
....

TAKING GOD SERIOUSLY
How does it feel to deeply love and care for people who don't understand your way of loving? Read **John 11:1–45**.

....

How do you think Martha and Mary felt when Jesus did not respond immediately to their urgent distress call?

....

Why was Jesus so troubled by the two grieving sisters and their sympathizers?

....

What was Jesus' strategy for dealing with Martha and Mary's crisis? Did it work?

....
....

HERE TODAY—HERE TOMORROW!
What is really happening when we don't recognize or understand Jesus' response to our distress calls? See what special insight and reassurance **Acts 18:9–10** offers.

....
....

Which "special agents" has God provided to guide, encourage, and protect you as a disciple of Jesus Christ? Make a list.

....
....

Whom are you guiding, encouraging, and protecting as a "special agent" of God? Make a list.

....
....

From one man He made every nation of men, that they should inhabit the whole earth; and He determined the times set for them and the exact places where they should live. God did this so that men would seek Him and perhaps reach out for Him and find Him, though He is not far from each one of us. Acts 17:26-27

31. Who Is the Greatest?

Matthew 18:1–9; 20:17–28

Lesson Focus

Teens need to know that God doesn't compare us to one another. God accepts each of us and reminds us that we are precious in His sight (Isaiah 43:4), in spite of our sin and apart from our "works."

WHO IS THE GREATEST? (10 minutes)

Distribute copies of the student page and ask students to share their selections. Note that students will probably not agree on their choices. We often argue about who is the greatest at something, because we all have different criteria for being great.

COMPARED TO YOU... (15 minutes)

Teenagers are very concerned about how they measure up to their peers. It's natural to compare oneself to someone else. In fact, that's how we often try to find our value and self-worth.

Ask students to list some of the things that men and women use to compare themselves to each other. Discuss what kinds of things the students feel are compared. Help students identify how comparing themselves to others can be positive and negative. (As a variation, you may want to divide students into separate groups of guys and gals and compare lists.)

IN THE WORD (20 minutes)

Ask the students to read Matthew 18:1–9 and 20:20–28. Allow students to work together in groups of two or three to answer the questions from the student page.

The disciples were like everyone else; they wanted to know where they fit into the kingdom of God.

The disciples were looking to see who among them was greater than all the rest; they did so by comparing themselves to one another.

Jesus desires more than just a change in behavior; He wants people to change the way they think about the kingdom of God.

Jesus wants everyone to be humble, loving, accepting, and to follow Him without question. He wants everyone for His own disciple.

Children do not love Jesus because they want to be great, but because Jesus loved them first. When Jesus draws believers to Himself, they go without question, loving Jesus and trusting Him completely.

The Scriptures tell us that the "last will be first, and the first will be last" (Matthew 20:16). Greatness is found in humbling oneself before God and realizing that only through the saving grace of God may we gain the reward of eternal life.

Have students read the passages from Philippians and respond to the question. The greatest attribute of Christ is His absolute humility before the Father. He willingly gave Himself up as sacrifice for the sins of all people in order to give us eternal life.

CLOSING (5 minutes)

Close with prayer. Allow students to share any prayer concerns that they may have.

LESSON EXTENDER

Have students make a list of some of the greatest people they have ever known or heard of in the Church, like Martin Luther, Mother Teresa, a favorite pastor, or a Sunday School teacher. As they think about these "great" people, have them identify what their best qualities were. How did they model servanthood? Did they exemplify any of the childlike qualities Jesus taught? How did they demonstrate these same qualities in their daily lives? Remind students that all great leaders are forgiven sinners empowered by God.

WHO IS THE GREATEST?

WHO IS THE GREATEST?
Who is the greatest musician today?

Who was the best president (prime minister) in the history of your country?

Who is the most impressive teacher at your school?

Who is the most productive home-run hitter in baseball?

Who was the most powerful general in world history?

COMPARED TO YOU . . .
We try to find value and self-worth by comparing ourselves to other people. What kinds of things do people compare?

Men:

Women:

How could this have a positive effect on a person?

How could this impact a person negatively?

IN THE WORD
Read **Matthew 18:1–9** and **20:20–28**.

Why would the disciples want to know who was the greatest in the kingdom of God?

What were the disciples really doing among themselves?

In **18:3**, what are we supposed to change? Who brings change in people's lives?

What qualities of a child are we supposed to exemplify?

Do children love Jesus in order to become great? Why do children love Jesus?

What makes a person great in the kingdom of God? How is that greatness rewarded?

Read **Philippians 2:5–11**. Who is truly the greatest in God's kingdom?

Journey of Faith © 2007 Concordia Publishing House. Reproduced by permission.

32. BLESS YOU!

Mark 10:13–16

Lesson Focus

Teenagers are still trying to "find themselves," trying to determine who they are. Yet it is more important to know whose they are. They are God's, and they are precious in His sight.

OH, GROW UP! (5 minutes)

We all have been accused of acting childishly at one time or another. Give an example (or two) of a time when you were told to "grow up." Then ask the students to share stories as well. If they are not willing to talk about themselves, ask for other examples that aren't about them (no names, of course).

CHILDREN OF THE HEAVENLY FATHER (10 minutes)

Distribute copies of the student page. Talk about the way children in Jesus' time were treated compared to today. Read Mark 10:13–16. Continue the discussion with the questions in this section.

TOUCHED BY JESUS (20 minutes)

Many people say that their favorite "picture" of Jesus is the painting in which Jesus is not only blessing the children, but also holding them in His arms on His lap. The image of Jesus as both elder Brother and as loving "Abba" Father is extremely comforting.

Divide the class into pairs or groups, and have them investigate the other examples of how Jesus brought healing and blessing to others. Then, help the students to give examples of ways in which Jesus has touched their lives with healing and blessing, starting with His ultimate sacrifice on the cross. Be sure to give examples from your own life.

WHO'S THE GREATEST? (15 minutes)

We are guilty of wanting to be first. Discuss Jesus' response to the disciples' childish behavior in Matthew 18:1–6. Brainstorm ways in which we can put the J-O-Y principle (Jesus-Others-You) into practice. Close this section with Gospel comfort so that they know that, when they don't do these things, Jesus has died on the cross so that God forgives us for Jesus' sake.

CLOSING (5 minutes)

Read Isaiah 40:11 together. Let your closing prayer reflect the image of Jesus as the tender Shepherd. Sing "I Am Jesus' Little Lamb" (*LSB* 740; *AGPS* 125), or "Children of the Heavenly Father" (*LSB* 725; *HS98* 888).

BLESS YOU!

CHILDREN OF THE HEAVENLY FATHER

Children in Jesus' time were nonentities; they were most definitely to be seen and not heard. Read **Mark 10:13–16**. How does the disciples' reaction compare with the situations you discussed earlier?

With what adjective does Mark describe Jesus' response to the disciples?

What does that tell you about Jesus?

TOUCHED BY JESUS

Reread **verse 16**. How does Jesus demonstrate His love for the children? How do you think that made them feel?

Read the following passages and talk about how Christ's touch brought healing and blessing to each of these people:

Matthew 8:3

Matthew 8:15

Matthew 9:29–30

Matthew 17:7

Mark 7:33–35

Luke 22:51

How has Jesus touched your life with healing and blessing?

WHO'S THE GREATEST?

Jesus wants us to be childlike, not childish. Read **Matthew 18:1–6**. How did Jesus respond to the childish behavior of the disciples?

How can we be more childlike and less childish?

Journey of Faith © 2007 Concordia Publishing House. Reproduced by permission.

33. Money Matters

Mark 14:3–9;
John 12:1–8

Lesson Focus

God demonstrated His love for us by giving His only Son in death for us. We respond in thanks to Him with our time, effort, and money.

OPENING (10 minutes)

Ask volunteers to choose between the options in each of the following sentences, explaining their choices:

Would you rather . . .

- have a secret admirer who gave you lots of presents or a best friend who shared everything with you?
- have lots of people with whom you are pretty good friends or a couple of friends to whom you are really close?
- give an expensive gift or receive one?

Point out the tension between giving and receiving, thanking and being thanked.

HOW DO YOU SPEND YOUR MONEY? (10 minutes)

Distribute copies of the student page. Have the students estimate how much money they spend on each of the listed items and how much they use in each category of the pie chart.

Tell the students, "How we spend our money can reflect our sinful nature. But it can also be a way of responding to the grace of God."

DIGGING IN (15 minutes)

Have the students read Mark 14:3–9. Explain that Jesus is on His way to Jerusalem to suffer and die. He stops in Bethany for dinner with Mary, Martha, and Lazarus. Discuss the questions from the student page. Suggested responses include

1. Mary may have known Jesus was headed to His death. She wanted Him to know how much she loved Him.
2. Money was apparently more important than Jesus to these people. Also ask, "How might this happen today?"
3. Jesus' ministry showed His love and concern for the poor (see Luke 4:18; 14:13; 18:22). The perfume symbolically prepared Jesus' body for death. Jesus meant that His death and resurrection were far more significant than money.
4. Yes. Jesus saw the real motives of people. Look at Mark 14:8. Jesus knew that Mary was expressing her love for Him.

EXPRESSING LOVE (10 minutes)

Have volunteers answer the questions. Then tell students that God's love for us moves us to express our love—to each other and back to God. Ask, "Why do these three things (money, time, and effort) show the depth of our love?" (The more money, time, and effort that we put in, the more we give of ourselves, showing that we care. Mary's gift to Jesus showed that she cared for Him deeply. Jesus could tell by knowing her heart; we can tell by observing her actions.)

A PLAN OF ACTION (5 minutes)

Have the students work through the remainder of the student page. Briefly discuss their responses. In 1 John 4:19, we learn that expressing love for each other is our response to what God first did for us. While love may not be our response according to our sinful nature, it is our response when moved by His great love for us. Help students identify ways they can express their love for God at home, church, and school. Encourage them to put their plan into action.

CLOSING (5 minutes)

Close with prayer, thanking God for His love and asking for the wisdom and discipline to express our love for God in all we do.

LESSON EXTENDER

✝ John's first epistle makes a distinction between "sinning" (unavoidable acts according to the sinful nature) and "being in sin" (allowing sin to reign in our lives). How does this make a difference in our lives?

Money Matters

HOW DO YOU SPEND YOUR MONEY?
List how much money you spend each week on the following:

Soda pop	_____
Clothes	_____
Entertainment (movies, games)	_____
Eating out	_____
Sports (watching and participating)	_____
Dating	_____
Other	_____
Total	_____

(Circle divided into sections labeled: God, Others, Savings, Yourself)

DIGGING IN
Read about a costly gift in **Mark 14:3–9**. Then respond to these questions:

1. We know that the woman who poured the perfume on Jesus was Mary (**John 12:3**). Why do you think she did this?

2. Why do you think some people complained about Mary spending so much money on Jesus?

3. Did Jesus not care about poor people? What did Jesus mean in **Mark 14:7–8**?

4. Did Jesus know why Mary poured the perfume on Him?

EXPRESSING LOVE
What kinds of things do people do to show they are in love? Don't such gifts include at least one of the following?
Money

Time

Careful planning and thoughtfulness

A PLAN OF ACTION
Look up **1 John 4:19**. Why do we love each other and God?

Because of sin, we would not choose to love God, if God had not first loved us. Our love is a Spirit-motivated response to His love for us. Mary used what she had to express her love for God. What things can we do to express our love for God?

STUDENT PAGE 33

Journey of Faith © 2007 Concordia Publishing House. Reproduced by permission.

34. Servant Leadership

John 13:1–20

Lesson Focus

The ultimate example of servant leadership is found in Jesus Christ, who willingly gives up His life for His followers.

OPENING (5 minutes)

Ask the students about the hardest job they ever did without receiving any pay. Did they volunteer to work without pay? Why did they do it? Transition by saying, "Today we look at an example of what it means to serve others and what it meant to give the ultimate sacrifice."

DIRTY FEET (15 minutes)

Select one or more volunteers to read aloud John 13:1–20. Allow time for students to answer individually the questions in this section. Discuss their insights. Answers will vary. Focus on the importance of understanding Jesus' role as a servant and how it contradicts our worldly view of leadership. Encourage students to personalize their thoughts about ways Christ serves us as He did the disciples.

WILLING SERVICE (15 minutes)

Have students take a look at verse 3. Discuss the questions as a whole group.

Answers might include that Jesus was showing love, the power of service, the last shall be first, how the Gospel turns the world on end, and so forth. Jesus spent His whole life serving others, such as the needy and poor, the broken and lost. He gave His life for all. Answers might include thinking of others first, helping to encourage others who struggle around us, and sharing the Gospel.

WILLING SACRIFICE (15 minutes)

Challenge students to complete the questions on their own. Discuss their answers as a whole group.

Jesus willingly set aside His power to become man. He experienced pain for us. He held back His power when tormented and killed. Christ took our place and did what we could not do. He did not just wash feet, but our sins are washed away with His blood and righteousness, which flowed from His nail-pierced hands.

Answers might include that He paid the ultimate price for His people; He gave us an example, as good leaders should do; and He gives us His Spirit to strengthen us for works of service.

CLOSING (5 minutes)

Ask a servant leader youth to serve by leading the prayer.

LESSON EXTENDER

Discuss how your students could be servant leaders in their community. What specific actions could they take to begin this process? Is a servant leader a "giver" or a "getter"? How?

Servant Leadership

DIRTY FEET
Read **John 13:1–20**.

Put yourself in the disciples' "shoes" as you answer the following questions:

What seems odd about this situation?

How would you react if Jesus wanted to wash your feet?

Compare your response to that of Peter.

What spiritual needs do you have that could be compared to dirty feet?

Design a sign to interpret Jesus' command to wash one another's feet.

WILLING SERVICE
Take a look at **verse 3**.

Why do you think Jesus lived such a humble and serving role if He knew that all power had been given to Him?

How did Jesus show servant leadership while on earth?

Who has demonstrated servant leadership to you? How?

How can we model servant leadership with those around us?

WILLING SACRIFICE
In Jesus, God became man. Consider the great sacrifice of an infinite God coming down to be a finite human. In that light, list the ways that Christ has been a servant to us.

How is the message of **John 13:1–20** similar to **John 19:16–18**?

The greatest leader is the one who gives the most. Make your case for Christ being the greatest leader ever.

Journey of Faith © 2007 Concordia Publishing House. Reproduced by permission.

STUDENT PAGE 34

35. THREE WORDS FROM THE CROSS

Luke 23:26–56

Lesson Focus

God is faithful to His promises. He is willing to forgive, demonstrating His great love for us.

THINKING ON THE CROSS (10 minutes)

Turn off all the lights in the room, and invite your students to get in a comfortable position, close their eyes, and try to form a mental picture of the crucifixion scene. Ask them to imagine what it's like. Allow for three minutes of silent meditation, and then ask students to share with the rest of the class what they see. Encourage them to give specific details as they visualize the scene.

Introduce the next section by saying something like, "However we picture it, the crucifixion scene had to be really ugly. Yet amidst all this ugliness, we see a true picture of God's love for us. Let's take a look at the Scriptures to see how this love is portrayed in Jesus' words from the cross."

THREE WORDS FOR THE THIEF (20 minutes)

Ask someone to read Luke 23:26–56 aloud while students follow along in their Bibles. Distribute copies of the student page. Ask your students to work individually, following the directions for this section.

Give students a few minutes to come up with symbols and try to complete the blanks. Before giving them the correct answers (WILLING, FOR, ABLE), ask students to imagine that they are the repentant thief on the cross. At first he cursed Jesus along with the other criminal (Matthew 27:44; Mark 15:32), but then he had a change of heart, asking Jesus to "remember" him. Have students think about the words of Jesus on the cross, and then ask them, "What was it that changed this man's heart?" Allow students to share their opinions. Conclude this section by saying something like, "From Jesus' words on the cross, the criminal learned that God is a forgiving God, and God was willing to forgive even him. When Jesus said to him, 'Today you will be with Me' (Luke 23:43), He was telling the thief that God's forgiveness was for him. And when Jesus committed Himself into His Father's hands, He showed the criminal that God is able to fulfill His promise, that God is faithful. Through Jesus' death on the cross for his sins, the thief learned that God was willing, God was for him, and God was able to give him forgiveness and eternal life.

THREE WORDS FOR ME (15 minutes)

Ask students to complete the next section on the student page individually. Invite volunteers to share their answers.

THREE WORDS FOR THE WORLD (10 minutes)

Ask students to think about where in the world people need to know God's forgiveness and promise of salvation through Jesus Christ. Remind students of local news events, world conflicts, friends, or relatives. Close by having a group prayer time, mentioning the specific situations that your students bring up.

LESSON EXTENDER

✝ Encourage students to keep a journal this week, recording how they have noticed that God is forgiving, that God blesses people, and that He is faithful.

✝ Ask your students to read Psalm 103. Invite them to pick out the various phrases the psalmist uses to show that God is forgiving, is faithful, and blesses His people.

THREE WORDS FROM THE CROSS

THREE WORDS FOR THE THIEF

In the space provided, draw a picture or symbol that represents Jesus' words. Then try to complete the blanks, telling what the thief learned about God by seeing Jesus on the cross.

> Father, forgive them

Luke 23:34 God is W ___ ___ ___ ___ ___ ___ to forgive the thief.

Luke 23:43 God's love is F ___ ___ the thief.

Luke 23:46 God is A ___ ___ ___ to save him.

THREE WORDS FOR ME

Jesus' words from the cross showed not only the thief but all of us that God is **willing** to forgive, God is **for** us, and God is **able** to save us all because His Son died for our sins. Take a moment to reflect on Jesus' words from the cross, and then complete the thoughts below with your own words. (For example, I know God is willing to forgive me because Jesus died in my place, which means He even forgives me when I am disrespectful toward my parents.)

I know God is **willing** to forgive me because . . . (See **John 3:16–17**.)

....

. . . which means He forgives . . .

....

I know God's love is **for** me because . . . (See **Romans 8:31–32**.)

....

. . . which means He is with me even when . . .

....

I know God is **able** to save me because . . . (See **Ephesians 3:20–21** and **Hebrews 7:25**.)

....

. . . which means I will be with Him even though . . .

....

STUDENT PAGE 35

Journey of Faith © 2007 Concordia Publishing House. Reproduced by permission.

36. New View of an Old Story

1 Corinthians 15:1–11

Lesson Focus

The "old story" of the crucifixion and resurrection are central events for our faith and have daily application in our lives.

SAME OLD STORY IN A NEW WAY (10 minutes)

Tell your class that they are going to retell the Easter story, but in a new way. Pick someone to start, and share the following "rules":

1. Each person may use only five words, and then it's the next person's turn.

2. You may not use any "to be" verbs (is, are, was, were, and so forth). The point is for students to think about what they want to say and focus on what's important to share in just five words. Introduce the next section by saying something like, "We just told the Easter story in a new way. Now, we want to look at that 'old story' in a new way, through the eyes of the apostle Paul, to see what it means for our lives today."

SO WHAT? (25 minutes)

Distribute copies of the student page. Direct students to look up the passage in their Bibles and fill in the blanks. Answers:

1. died for our sins
2. buried
3. raised on the third day
4. Peter, the Twelve
5. more than five hundred
6. James, all the apostles, me

As they fill in the blanks, ask students to answer the three corresponding "So what?" questions. Give students about ten minutes to work on their answers, and then ask them to share their responses with the rest of the class.

SO WHAT ABOUT EASTER TODAY? (10 minutes)

Rather than telling the traditional Easter story, Paul in 1 Corinthians 15 lists a series of facts as of "first importance." To Paul these were critical, life-changing facts with power for everyday living.

Ask students to pick one of the facts that Paul lists in this passage as the most important to them right now in their lives and the reason for its importance. For example, a student might choose "raised on the third day" (verse 4) and say something like, "It gives me hope that I, too, will be raised, and this life is not all there is."

SO WHAT ABOUT OTHERS? (10 minutes)

To close, ask your students to think about friends they have who either do not know Jesus or who know the facts of the story, but they don't seem to make any difference in their lives. Encourage students to pick one of the facts that might apply to their lives and pray for an opportunity to share with that friend, using a prayer similar to this.

"Dear Jesus, please help me to share with (friend's name) the fact that You (died for his sin, rose on the third day, and so forth) that he might know You and the eternal life You give. In Your name I pray. Amen."

LESSON EXTENDER

✝ Invite students to look up parallel passages of the Easter story in the Gospels (Matthew 28:1–15; Mark 16:1–8; Luke 24:1–35; John 20:1–23) to compare and contrast what each author included in his telling of the events.

✝ Ask students to send a "Happy Easter" e-mail greeting card (even if it's not Easter) sharing the basics of the Easter message and a note of God's love to a friend.

New View of an Old Story

SO WHAT?

Take a look at **1 Corinthians 15:3–7**. Fill in the blanks below according to the facts Paul lists in the passage. Then ask yourself, "So what?" and answer the three questions under each one.

According to the Scriptures,

(Verse 3) Christ _____ _____ ____ _____.

So what?
Why do you think this is included?

....

Why does Paul say it is "of first importance"?

....

Why is it important for me to know and believe?

....

(Verse 4) He was _____.

So what?
Why do you think this is included?

....

Why does Paul say it is "of first importance"?

....

Why is it important for me to know and believe?

....

(Verse 4) He was _____ _____ _____ _____ _____.

So what?
Why do you think this is included?

....

Why does Paul say it is "of first importance"?

....

Why is it important for me to know and believe?

....

(Verse 5) He appeared to _____, then to _____ _____.

So what?
Why do you think this is included?

....

Why does Paul say it is "of first importance"?

....

Why is it important for me to know and believe?

....

(Verse 6) He appeared to _____ _____ _____ _____.

So what?
Why do you think this is included?

....

Why does Paul say it is "of first importance"?

....

Why is it important for me to know and believe?

....

(Verse 7) He appeared to _____, then to _____ _____ _____, and last of all to _____.

So what?
Why do you think this is included?

....

Why does Paul say it is "of first importance"?

....

Why is it important for me to know and believe?

....

Journey of Faith © 2007 Concordia Publishing House. Reproduced by permission.

STUDENT PAGE 36

37. Miraculous Fishing and Love

John 21:1–25

Lesson Focus

In this session, the students will know that God provides for them in miraculous ways, especially when it comes to their salvation.

OPENING (5 minutes)

Ask students to talk about their most memorable fishing trip (if any). Did they catch any fish? Did the big one get away? Talk about the different kinds of fishing (deep sea fishing, fly fishing, lake fishing) they may have experienced.

THINKING ABOUT MIRACLES (15 minutes)

Distribute copies of the student page. Challenge students to think about the different miracles in the Old and New Testaments. Have students record which Bible miracle they think was the most spectacular. Discuss the students' choices. Why did they select the miracles that they did? The most miraculous thing that affects us personally is that, despite the fact that we are sinful and unfaithful, God still loves us (see Romans 5:6–8).

THE MIRACLES IN JOHN 21 (20 minutes)

Ask volunteers to read John 21:1–25 aloud, or have the students read it as a drama.

Ask the students to identify the two major miracles that occurred in this lesson (the miraculous catch of fish, the miraculous love shown to Peter).

Ask a student to reread verses 15–17. Then challenge the students to honestly answer the next question. You might start by suggesting that your actions certainly don't always show Him that you love Him all the time.

Get students thinking about God's miraculous love. St. Paul reminds us that "while we were still sinners, Christ died for us" (Romans 5:8). He loves you despite the things you think, say, or do. Your salvation is sure (Ephesians 2:8–9).

SHARING THE MIRACLES (10 minutes)

Remind the students that God performs some of His miraculous deeds through us. Ask the students to identify the clear command God gives to Peter and to us ("feed My lambs"). Let the students list some specific things they can do this week to carry out this command. Discuss these ways. Encourage them to add additional things to their list as they share in class.

CLOSING (5 minutes)

Invite the students to join in prayer, thanking God for His constant love for them and asking for power to carry out the command of sharing that love with others. Encourage them to pray specifically for help to do the things they have listed on their worksheets.

LESSON EXTENDER

✝ Ask students to interview a full-time church worker. They can ask, "Why did you decide on this profession? What are the joys and sorrows of church work?" These interviews could be shared at the next class.

✝ Ask students to jot a note or card to someone they know who has a special need to hear of God's love. Encourage them to specifically tell of God's love shown in the sending of His Son, Jesus Christ, to redeem that person for eternity.

Miraculous Fishing and Love

THINKING ABOUT MIRACLES

The most spectacular miracle in the Bible was the time when . . .

....
....
....
....
....
....
....
....
....
....
....
....
....
....

THE MIRACLES IN JOHN 21

Identify the two miracles in **John 21:1–20**.

....

Read **John 21:15–17**. Suppose Jesus asked you the same question He asked Peter. How would you answer?

A. Of course, I love You, Lord. All the time.

B. Well, once in a while.

C. I try to love You, but I know I don't always.

D. Never.

What is miraculous about God's love?

1. Romans 5:8

....
....
....
....

2. Ephesians 2:8–9

....
....
....
....

SHARING THE MIRACLES

What clear command does Jesus give to Peter—and to each of us—in **verses 15–17**?

....
....

List some specific things we can do this week to carry out this command.

....
....

Journey of Faith © 2007 Concordia Publishing House. Reproduced by permission.

38. Ignited by God's Word

Luke 24:13–35

Lesson Focus

God establishes faith according to His plan. He creates faith in us and nurtures it with His Word and Sacraments so we may have eternal life through Jesus Christ.

FIRESIDE CHAT (10 minutes)

Ask your students to orally list the qualities of fire. Starting with the student closest to you, have each person name one quality, without thinking too long about their answer. Their list may include words such as *burning, consuming, spreads, needs fuel*, and so forth. Now ask students to list the qualities of the faith the Holy Spirit gives us through God's grace. Their list should include similar adjectives. Discuss how our faith from the Holy Spirit is ignited by God's Word and leads to eternal life with our heavenly Father.

IGNITED (20 minutes)

Distribute copies of the student page. Read the verses from Luke and discuss the questions. Jesus knew Cleopas and his companion had placed their hope in Him. They were miserable because they believed He was dead. Through divine intervention these men were unable to recognize Jesus. Before revealing Himself to them, Jesus taught them about the suffering He had to endure as the true Messiah.

By God's grace we receive faith from the Holy Spirit according to God's plan. Now that Jesus had explained what the Scriptures taught about Him (Luke 24:25–27), these men were ready for faith. They saw that God's plan was not ruined by Jesus' death, but rather accomplished by it.

Cleopas and his companion walked seven miles back to Jerusalem to share the good news that Jesus had risen from the dead. The Holy Spirit still gives modern believers burning faith. Just like fire naturally gives off heat, we can't help but share our faith with others when the Holy Spirit burns inside our hearts. We are ignited by God's Word.

NURTURED (15 minutes)

Allow students to work with one or two others to read the suggested verses and answer the question. Review as a whole group. The Holy Spirit plants and nurtures the seed of faith. In Matthew 13:3–8, Jesus shares a parable that shows us as the sower spreading God's Word and the Holy Spirit creating faith. The mustard seed (Matthew 13:31–32) is God's Word; although it starts tiny, by God's grace, it will eventually spread throughout the world. In John 15:1–8, we learn that, when we are out of contact with God's Word, we are lifeless. The good news is that Jesus promises to remain in us.

CLOSING (5 minutes)

Close with prayer, thanking God for the faith He gives, which begins with His Word and spreads to eternal life with Him. Ask Him to nurture the seed of faith in your heart to help you spread the good news of His love.

LESSON EXTENDER

✞ Read the explanation of the Third Article of the Apostles' Creed in Luther's Small Catechism to reinforce that all faith comes from God.

IGNITED BY GOD'S WORD

IGNITED
Read **Luke 24:13–19**.

What was upsetting the men, and why did Jesus ask about it if He already knows everything?

....
....
....
....

Read **Luke 24:30–32**.

How were these men able to recognize Jesus now?

....
....
....

Read **Luke 24:32–35**.

Why did the two men go back to Jerusalem after Jesus revealed Himself to them?

....
....
....

Who provides this burning faith for us today, thousands of years after Jesus' resurrection?

....
....
....

What is our response to having faith?

....
....
....

NURTURED
By God's grace the Holy Spirit plants and nurtures the seed of faith. Read these verses and record your summaries of God's message related to the life-giving faith of the Holy Spirit. Be prepared to share your responses with the rest of the group.

Matthew 13:3–8

....
....
....
....

Matthew 13:31–32

....
....
....

John 15:1–8, especially **verse 4**

....
....
....

STUDENT PAGE 38

Journey of Faith © 2007 Concordia Publishing House. Reproduced by permission.

39. I'M SUPPOSED TO DO WHAT?

Matthew 28:16–20

Lesson Focus

The Great Commission would be overwhelming, but our Lord also gives us the plan and the power to accomplish His purpose!

OPENING (10 minutes)

Have a world map and a map of your own area. Make a short list of relatively obscure places. Have students find the places on the world map. Make a short list of places or streets in your area. Have students find these places on the map. Ask how many people in the class have been to each of the places.

Read Matthew 28:16–20. Ask which of the places was included in the command of Jesus to make disciples of all nations. Discuss whether it is easier to witness to people you know or to people you don't know.

A QUESTION OF AUTHORITY (5 minutes)

Allow students to complete this section on their own. Review with the whole group. Students would probably be more likely to obey their mom or dad than their younger brother. Parents are in positions of authority, whereas the younger brother is not.

In Matthew 28:18 Jesus says, "All authority in heaven and on earth has been given to Me." Jesus is able to act with authority because He has all authority.

DEPUTIZING DISCIPLES (5 minutes)

Complete this section with the whole group. With the way the statement is phrased in verse 19, Jesus speaks directly to the disciples whom He had called and trained. Because Jesus has ultimate authority, He gives the command to go. It is similar to a sheriff deputizing officers to assist in his work. The disciples, in turn, would preach and teach others, who would be called into the ministry by the Church. They then would tell others and so on.

The statement Jesus makes is direct and is a command. It is also active and specific. If Jesus had simply said, "Therefore let people know about Me," one could possibly excuse sitting back with an attitude that people can ask about Jesus if they want to know.

HERE'S THE PLAN (5 minutes)

Continue to work on this section as a whole group. Jesus in His wisdom did not simply give us a command to go and make disciples of all nations and then leave us to our own devices to accomplish the task. He states specifically that this should be done by baptizing and by teaching. Essentially, making disciples is done through the Word and Sacrament.

WHO? ME? (15 minutes)

Have students work individually to complete this section. Review with the whole group. Talking to people directly about one's faith is very often intimidating, for adults and teens alike. Discuss why this might be the case. Perhaps it creates vulnerability because we think of faith as such a personal thing. Perhaps it is simply Satan playing on our insecurities. There may be other reasons that contribute to the problem.

Thankfully, once again, the Lord doesn't leave us on our own. In the second part of verse 20, Jesus gives the assurance of His constant presence, both in the present and continuing until the end of time. We share God's Word, which He gives us, and point people toward His true Church. Close with prayer.

I'm Supposed to Do What?

A QUESTION OF AUTHORITY

Would you be more likley to take out the trash if your mom or dad told you to do it or if your younger brother told you to do it? Why?

....
....
....

Reread **Matthew 28:18**. What does Jesus say has been given to Him?

....
....
....

DEPUTIZING DISCIPLES

Reread **Matthew 28:19**. This is a command statement. To whom is Jesus speaking?

....
....

How might the meaning change if Jesus had said, "Therefore let people know about Me"?

....
....
....

HERE'S THE PLAN

Jesus does not simply say to make disciples of all nations; He also says how it is to be done. What are the two main ways Jesus says to make disciples?

1. ....
....

2. ....
....

WHO? ME?

Have you ever talked to anyone directly about Jesus? If yes, how did you feel right before you started? If no, how does the thought of doing it make you feel?

....
....

It certainly is a big task that Jesus commands to be done. It could easily be daunting and overwhelming. Read the second part of **Matthew 28:20**. What is the assurance Jesus gives?

....
....
....

What are three of the most powerful things you can think of? What are their capabilities? Remember, the Lord is more powerful than that—and He's on your side!

1. ....
....

2. ....

3. ....

Created in Christ © 2006 Concordia Publishing House. Scripture: NIV®. Reproduced by permission.

STUDENT PAGE 39

40. What Did You Say?

Acts 2:1–41;
Joel 2:28–29;
John 16:5–11

Lesson Focus

The Holy Spirit continues to empower our relationship with God by helping us to gladly hear and understand God's Word.

SAY WHAT? (10 minutes)

Distribute copies of the student page. Ask students to think about the way they talk. Do they sometimes slip into slang? Do they use a lot of "verbal garbage" ("er," "you know," "um," "like," "ah")? What does the expression "huh?" mean? When or why is it used?

HUH? (15 minutes)

Students may need help to understand about the Holy Spirit. People two thousand years ago didn't get it, either. Peter tried to explain after some of the crowd mocked the disciples.

Read the Bible passages and discuss the questions. Suggested responses:

Some people suggested that the disciples were drunk.

Joel spoke of a time when the Holy Spirit would rest upon all people, not just the prophets.

Peter pled his case by speaking of the death and resurrection of Christ. Peter talked about David, who was respected by Peter's audience, and who looked forward to the Messiah.

The people began to listen when their hearts were touched; God's Word caused repentance and desire for God's forgiveness.

After Peter heard and saw how God's Word had touched the people, he proclaimed the gift of God's grace that comes through Baptism.

The people gladly received the Word and were baptized.

LISTEN UP (20 minutes)

Have the class read John 16:5–11. The Holy Spirit acts to counsel us in our faith (i.e., to produce, enable, and grow faith within us).

The Holy Spirit encourages us in our faith, helps us learn and understand God's Word, helps us make sense of God's Law and Gospel, sustains our relationship with God, and gives us courage to live out our faith.

Ask students if listening or speaking is more important. How and when can either action be taken for granted?

Ask students to reflect about their lives. When are they silent? What are they saying when they open their mouths?

What is the role of our tongue in our relationship with God? How can our mouths be used to serve Him?

When can they be a coach, teacher, helper, lawyer, or friend for Christ?

CLOSING (5 minutes)

Close in prayer, asking God to guide the students as they speak and listen. Be sure to include any specific prayer requests that students may have.

LESSON EXTENDER

✝ Ask students to keep a one-week record of what they say (what, when, where, how, and to whom). Does their tongue increase their sense of marvel, closeness, distance, and/or conflict in relationship with others?

WHAT DID YOU SAY?

SAY WHAT?

Have you ever tried counting how many times you've said "huh?" or "what?" in a single day? Did you just say "huh?" when you read the last sentence? "Huh?" is a request for clarification, an essential part of completing the communication loop. If it were not for the vitally important "Huh?" we would often be left in the dark or unable to function. "Huh?" is difficult to live without. In what circumstances do you say it more often?

- ☐ With teachers?
- ☐ With friends?
- ☐ With siblings?
- ☐ With parents?
- ☐ With grandparents?
- ☐ With relatives?

HUH?

Imagine the possibility of being so "with it" that you see God's promise being fulfilled right before your eyes! What thoughts might be going through your head?

Read **Acts 2:1–12**. The people were amazed and confused.

How were the disciples mocked (**verse 13**)?

What did Peter mean when he stood up and explained that they all had witnessed the fulfillment of the prophet Joel (**verses 14–21**)?

What else did Peter say in response (**verses 22–24**)? How was the history of God's people important to this message (**verses 25–36**)?

How did the people respond (**verses 36–37**)?

What did Peter proclaim about the way God works to save repentant sinners (**verses 38–40**)?

How did the people respond (**verse 41**)?

LISTEN UP

The Holy Spirit is also referred to as the Comforter. A comforter listens to you and cares for you deeply.

Read **John 16:5–11**.

What is the job of the Holy Spirit in **verse 7**?

How is the Spirit like a coach? teacher? lawyer? friend? helper?

STUDENT PAGE 40

Journey of Faith © 2007 Concordia Publishing House. Reproduced by permission.

41. Rejoicing in God's Power

Acts 3:1–13;
4:1–31;
1 Peter 1:3–9

Lesson Focus

God gave Peter and John the power to heal. He satisfies our earthly and eternal needs; He gives us faith that leads us to praise Him.

THANKSGIVING (10 minutes)

Have students work with a partner to list orally the blessings God has given them. Suggest they concentrate on those categories listed in Luther's explanation of the First Article of the Apostles' Creed (family, health, possessions, etc.). Ask one partner from each pair to report some of the blessings they listed. Encourage students to name items others haven't already mentioned. Emphasize that God provides us with all our needs. He gives us faith to praise Him, which is our response to His power and goodness.

HEALING IN JESUS' NAME (10 minutes)

Distribute copies of the student page and read together Acts 3:1–13; 4:1–31. Discuss that the beggar was crippled from birth so he was carried to the temple courts, where he pleaded for alms. The beggar asked Peter and John for money; instead, they healed him and gave him the Good News of Jesus Christ and forgiveness of all his sins. He was so joyful that he went with Peter and John around the temple courts praising God. The rest of the people were amazed and wondered about God; some believed and praised Him.

POWERFUL PROVIDER (15 minutes)

Have students work again with their partner to review the verses and questions in this section. Summarize with the whole group. God promises to fulfill our needs, just as He gave Peter and John the ability to heal and restore the crippled beggar's health. In Matthew 6:25, 33, God promises to provide for us, and therefore we have no reason to worry. Matthew 7:7–11 reminds us that God is our heavenly Father who satisfies us. Paul writes in 2 Corinthians 1:10–11 that God also fulfills our spiritual needs by delivering us from sin. Our response for this freedom is praise and thanksgiving.

OUR PRAISE (10 minutes)

God is certainly able and often does give much more than we ask for or imagine. For example, when the beggar wanted a better earthly life, God graciously gave him eternal life through faith in Christ Jesus. The healed beggar couldn't help but praise God.

Our hope is in Christ, whose life and resurrection give us salvation. We praise Him because He has given us indescribable and glorious joy.

CLOSING (5 minutes)

Have the students pray silently by themselves; you might suggest they find a quiet area of the room in which to pray. Encourage students to confess to God situations in which they have trouble trusting in Him. Then ask Him for specific requests on their hearts. End their prayer by thanking God for being their Comforter, Good Shepherd, Savior, and so forth.

LESSON EXTENDER

✝ Discuss ways we can become more aware of how God works in our lives. Ask your students to keep a "Thanks" journal this week in which every day they list the blessings God gives them. Remind students to include the daily blessing of His Word.

Rejoicing in God's Power

HEALING IN JESUS' NAME
Read **Acts 3:1–13; 4:1–31** to answer these questions.

Why was the lame man begging at the temple?

What did Peter and John give him, and how did this change the beggar?

POWERFUL PROVIDER
Summarize in your own words the promise given to us in each of these verses. What is our response?

Matthew 6:25, 33

Matthew 7:7–11

2 Corinthians 1:10–11

OUR PRAISE
God provides us with all our needs. By His grace and the faith He gives us through His Son, Jesus Christ, we praise Him.

Read **Ephesians 3:20–21**.

What does this verse say about the way God answers prayer? How do you think the beggar in the story felt about God giving much more than he asked for or imagined?

Read **1 Peter 1:3–9**.

What does our new birth in Christ mean?

STUDENT PAGE 41

Journey of Faith © 2007 Concordia Publishing House. Reproduced by permission.

42. To-Do List

Acts 6:1–8:1

Lesson Focus

Students will learn that, as God sustains and increases His Church here on earth, He provides many opportunities for service.

OPENING (5 minutes)

Before class, gather items from your church that are used by various workers. For example, a Bible from the pastor, a computer printout from the secretary, music from the organist, a kitchen utensil from the ladies' service group, and a cleaning tool from the janitor. Try to include items that might not be obviously identified as used for "church" tasks. (If you aren't familiar with the workers in your congregation, speak to the pastor or another leader ahead of time to find out about what is being done by whom.)

Show the items one by one, asking who uses them and discussing what that person's job might entail. Have students think about other workers within your congregation and what services they provide.

WHAT CAN I DO? (10 minutes)

Distribute copies of the student page. Encourage students to write a list of services performed within your congregation. Have volunteers share their lists. Encourage students to add ideas from one another's lists. Discuss the questions on the student page. Help students to see that they are capable of service at this point in their lives.

WHY CAN I HELP? (20 minutes)

Have students read Acts 6:1–7 and answer the first two questions. Stress the fact that helping others meet physical needs is an important way to share God's love. It may lead to opportunities to share the Gospel.

Have students take turns reading Acts 6:8–7:53. Explain beforehand that this section is Stephen's statement of self-defense, explaining why he was willing to risk his life to preach the Gospel. He retold Old Testament history and chastised those who rejected Christ—the Righteous One. You may want to divide the reading and have students report on specific sections.

Work through the next two questions, stressing that God gives His children strength and power to work for Him.

Read Acts 7:54–8:1. As the class answers the last two questions, focus on how God gave Stephen a strong faith and concern for others.

HOW CAN I HELP? (10 minutes)

Ask students to work through this section. Volunteers may share their plans. Help students identify contact people to help them get started. Be ready to offer suggestions to those who struggle.

As you finish, remind students that their works of service for Christ and His Church also help spread the news of His saving love. Their strength and ability to serve come from God. He will support and guide their efforts.

CLOSING (5 minutes)

Close with a prayer thanking God for the workers in your church. Include several by name. Then allow time for students to silently pray about their own plans for service.

LESSON EXTENDER

✝ Have various congregational workers speak to your students and share information about their work for the church.

✝ Develop and carry out a group project designed to meet a need within your congregation.

To-Do List

WHAT CAN I DO?

Make a list of jobs that can be or need to be done at your church.
Which jobs require special talent or training?
What abilities and talents has God given you that you could use to serve Him in your church?
Put an X by each job that you might be able to do.

Jobs	Talent/Training	I'm Qualifed

WHY CAN I HELP?

We learn in Acts that, as the Early Church grew, more opportunities for service became available. Read **Acts 6:1–7**. What job was Stephen chosen to do?

Why was this job important?

Read **Acts 6:8–7:53**. Because Stephen had an opportunity to serve the people, he also had an opportunity to witness the Gospel. Through whose power was Stephen able to speak (**Acts 6:10**)?

Read **1 Corinthians 12:4–7**. Why does the Holy Spirit give us power to work and speak for Him? Stephen lived to serve God. Read **Acts 7:54–8:1**. How did Stephen's earthly life end?

According to the Bible, what were his final two requests (**verses 59 and 60**)?

1.

2.

HOW CAN I HELP?

Pick one or two of the jobs you listed in part 1. Plan a way in which you can become involved in that service to the Church.

Do you need more information or skills?

Whom do you need to contact to become involved?

What can you do to be of service right now? Who gives you the strength and ability to serve?

STUDENT PAGE 42

43. SEARCHING FOR WHOLENESS

Acts 8:26–40

Lesson Focus

As they move toward adulthood, young people seek independence, self-identity, and purpose. Our sinful nature would misdirect our search. The Good News is that God seeks us out, through His Son, to give us new life and wholeness.

FOR WHAT ARE YOU SEARCHING? (15 minutes)

Distribute copies of the student page. Invite students, in teams or as a group, to build a list of things people search for. There will be all kinds of answers: money, sex, love, career, cars, houses, adventure, and others. Be sure to highlight redemption, belonging, hope, meaning, and God.

Then allow the students to identify things *they* search for. Do not require sharing, but allow volunteers to share, especially items not on the first list.

SEARCHING IN SCRIPTURE (20 minutes)

Read, or have a volunteer read, the introductory sentence and **Acts 8:26–40**. Then discuss the questions, making these points:

1. Clearly the Ethiopian was trying to find God. His search may have been fueled by his physical condition. As a eunuch, he was deformed and less than whole. He may have wondered if such a person could find peace with God. This is our question, too, for no one is perfect in body or spirit. The Ethiopian was reading from the Jewish Bible, but he was not understanding. Ask, "How can a person like the Ethiopian learn about religion, but not know God?" (Religion can be a way of searching for God, but what we truly need is for God to search for us!)

2. It may take your students a moment to realize that Jesus was right there, searching for the Ethiopian! Through Philip, God showed the Ethiopian the connection between the Word he was reading and Baptism.

3. Philip, in response to God's messenger, searched for the Ethiopian. In finding him, Philip also found part of his own purpose in life.

MY SEARCH (15 minutes)

Invite the students to identify with either Philip or the Ethiopian. (You may wish to process this question in pairs or triads.) Like the Ethiopian, the students may be searching. Point out that Philip was searching at one point in his life, too. (See John 1:43–45.) God by His grace moves those who are dead in sin to "seek" Him. He turns "seekers" into those who seek others for Him.

In Baptism, the Ethiopian received forgiveness and a sense of wholeness found only in God, who cares for us. He was freed, in a sense, from his incompleteness because Jesus gave him what he truly needed. Jesus does the same for us, of course. Go back to the list students created at the beginning of the study. Point out that God, through our Baptism and new life, can give us so much of what we're searching for.

There will be things on the list that God may not provide. It may be that God has a better time or way to respond to our search for those things. Nonetheless, we have a God who cares. He has found each one of us and continues to love us.

CLOSING (5 minutes)

Invite the students to compose a brief prayer of thanks for one of the blessings God provides. (They could use the back of the student page.) Let volunteers share their prayers for the closing.

LESSON EXTENDER

✞ Ask the students, "Is there a Philip in your life—someone who has helped you find spiritual wholeness?" Invite them to write prayers of thanks for the people they identify.

Searching for Wholeness

FOR WHAT ARE YOU SEARCHING?

People are searching for a lot of different things in life. List as many as you can think of.

Which three things on the list are most important to you right now? Why?

1. ....
2. ....
3. ....
4. ....
5. ....
6. ....
7. ....
8. ....
9. ....
10. ....

SEARCHING IN SCRIPTURE

Read **Acts 8:26–40**. The Ethiopian had traveled a long way from home searching for something.

1. What do you think he was searching for? What had he found as of the time Philip met him?

   ....
   ....

2. Where was Jesus in this lesson? (For a hint, see **Matthew 28:20**.) What was Jesus searching for?

   ....
   ....

3. What was Philip searching for? Did he find it?

   ....
   ....

MY SEARCH

Who are you most like in your life right now—Philip? Or the Ethiopian? Why?

....
....
....
....
....

How did Baptism give the Ethiopian what he was searching for?

....
....
....

How does it give us what we are looking for?

....
....
....

Journey of Faith © 2007 Concordia Publishing House. Reproduced by permission.

44. It's a God Thing

Acts 9:1–20

Lesson Focus

God works in our daily lives changing and renewing us through the death and resurrection of Jesus.

ONE THING I'D CHANGE (10 minutes)

Ask students to complete this section. Ask students to share their responses with the class.

Ask, "Of all the answers you've shared, which do you think is the hardest to change and why?" Say, "Today we're going to see someone whose life was changed in an incredible way and how God can bring positive changes into our own lives."

ONE THING GOD CHANGED (25 minutes)

Direct your students' attention to the "Before and After" activity on the student page. Read the summary statements of how Saul was before and after his encounter with Jesus. Ask your students what happened, specifically, that changed Saul.

After they've shared their thoughts, assign various students "parts" for a dramatic reading of Acts 9:1–20. You will need a narrator, Jesus (the Lord), Saul, and Ananias. Encourage students to get into their parts so the story comes alive through their reading while the rest of the class follows along in their Bibles.

In other places in the New Testament, Paul describes himself before meeting Jesus as pretty much being on top of the world (Philippians 3:4–6). From what we read here, was Saul looking to change his ways and his life? (No.)

Do you think Paul even wanted to change? (No.)

So, if Paul wasn't looking to change and didn't even want to, what happened? (God happened! He came crashing into Paul's life.)

Ask, "Why do you think this doesn't happen to everyone?"

Explain that there isn't one reason why some people change dramatically and some seem to be not affected at all. The focus really isn't on what people do, but on what God does. Saul could have never changed from sinner to saint, persecutor to preacher, hater of God to lover of Jesus, without God revealing His love and forgiveness to him through Jesus Christ. The same is true of each one of us. Without Jesus' death on the cross for our sins and His rising from the dead to give us new life, we have no power to change. What makes us change is the Holy Spirit working according to God's promises.

A GOD THING FOR ME (10 minutes)

Direct your students' attention to the Bible verses printed at the bottom of the student page. Point out that Saul's change was not by his will, strength, or decision, but by God's power. So through His Word and Sacraments, God promises us power to change. Ask students to select one of the verses and share what it says to them about God's life-changing power. Close by having each student read their passage aloud as a closing prayer.

LESSON EXTENDER

✝ Invite students to write the passages they selected on 3 x 5 index cards and carry them to memorize during the week.

✝ Ask them to pick another person in the class to pray for this week, sending them a note of encouragement by mail or e-mail during the week.

It's a God Thing

ONE THING I'D CHANGE

Complete the sentences below.

One thing I'd change about the world is . . .

....

....

....

One thing I'd change about my family is . . .

....

....

....

One thing I'd change about myself is . . .

....

....

....

ONE THING GOD CHANGED

Saul B.C. (Before meeting Christ)

☐ Hated Christians **(Acts 9:1)**

☐ Dragged men and women believers into prison **(Acts 8:3)**

☐ Approved of the stoning death of Stephen **(Acts 8:1)**

☐ Was generally a no-good, nasty, evil fellow **(1 Timothy 1:13)**

Saul (Paul) A.C. (After Christ came to him)

☐ Began preaching about God's love in Jesus Christ

☐ Was beaten, whipped, and stoned because of his Christian message

☐ Was exposed to death and constant danger because of his faith

☐ Endured hunger, thirst, cold, sleeplessness, and a lot of other nasty stuff in order to preach the Gospel **(2 Corinthians 11:23–27)**

A GOD THING FOR ME

2 Thessalonians 1:11–12
With this in mind, we constantly pray for you, that our God may count you worthy of His calling, and that by His power He may fulfill every good purpose of yours and every act prompted by your faith.

1 Thessalonians 5:23–24
May God Himself, the God of peace, sanctify you through and through. May your whole spirit soul and body be kept blameless at the coming of our Lord Jesus Christ. The one who calls you is faithful and He will do it.

Philippians 1:6
Being confident of this, that He who began a good work in you will carry it on to completion until the day of Christ Jesus.

Philippians 2:13
For it is God who works in you to will and to act according to His good purpose.

Journey of Faith © 2007 Concordia Publishing House. Reproduced by permission. Scripture: NIV®.

45. BEING BOLD

Acts 9:20–31; 13:1–33

Lesson Focus

Young people have many opportunities to tell of Christ's love to the people around them. The aim of this lesson is to help them see opportunities to be bold witnesses for God and His Church.

OPENING (5 minutes)

Ask the group to brainstorm ways people reveal they are Christians. Have a recorder write the examples on a chalkboard or newsprint. You may want to get the group started by giving examples.

SHOWING THE FAITH (10 minutes)

Distribute copies of the student page. Allow the students time to fill in their personal responses. Ask volunteers to share specific ways and times they let others see their faith.

Ask, "Is it always easy to show yourself as a Christian?" Discuss student answers, acknowledging difficulties and reminding them of the powerful help provided by the Holy Spirit.

STUDYING THE WORD (10 minutes)

In pairs or small groups, have the students read the passages and work through the questions. To avoid confusion, remind them that Saul's name was later changed to Paul.

When you bring the group back together, ask for responses to the first set of questions on the student page. Reinforce the idea that Paul's ministry was at times very difficult, yet God moved him to continue.

Reread Acts 13:16 to the group. Ask, "Whom is Paul talking to?" (Primarily the Jews.) "Why does he recount their history?" (He starts with what they already know. Then he takes the opportunity to build on that.)

SHARING THE GOSPEL (20 minutes)

Remind the students that Paul, led by the Holy Spirit, chose his words carefully as he witnessed to people. The Holy Spirit empowers us to do the same. We probably would not witness about Christ to everyone in exactly the same way. God helps us to pick appropriate approaches and times.

Work through the examples on the student page one at a time. Reinforce the fact that not all witnessing opportunities and approaches are identical.

Then ask the students, "What one thing stays the same in all these situations?" (We proclaim that we are saved by grace through Christ's death and resurrection.)

Read and discuss Matthew 28:19. God's command that we make disciples of all people is possible only by the power of the Holy Spirit.

CLOSING (5 minutes)

Ask students to once again think of ways they can show, in their speech and actions, that they are Christians. After allowing a silent minute or two for this, ask them to silently think of times this week when they will be able to put those ideas into action. Reread Matthew 28:19 to the group and close in prayer.

LESSON EXTENDER

✝ Have students role-play the situations presented in section 3.

✝ Ask students to make a list this week of the specific ways they see people showing and sharing their faith. Share these next week.

94

Being Bold

SHOWING THE FAITH

We see and hear the faith of God's people in many ways. How do *your* actions show *your* faith?

....
....
....
....

When might you be given opportunities to show your faith? List some specific examples:

....
....
....
....

STUDYING THE WORD

Read **Acts 9:20–31** and **Acts 13:1–12**.

What problems did Saul (Paul) face in his ministry? Why can telling about God be difficult?

....
....
....

What can make it easier? How was Paul's ministry blessed?

....
....
....

Read **Acts 13:13–33**. Whom is Paul talking to? Why does he recount their history?

....
....
....
....

SHARING THE GOSPEL

How might you witness to

a little child?

....

a very sick elderly neighbor?

....

a non-Christian friend from school?

....

a friend whose faith seems weak?

....

a person who tries to convert you to a non-Christian religion?

....

What one thing stays the same in all these situations?

....
....

What is God's command to us in **Matthew 28:19**? How can we possibly do that?

....
....
....

Journey of Faith © 2007 Concordia Publishing House. Reproduced by permission.

46. ENERGIZED ENCOURAGERS!

Acts 4:32–37; Acts 11:19–30

Lesson Focus

Barnabas was an "Energized Encourager" in the Early Church. In his life, we can see God's encouragement for us too.

ENCOURAGING WORDS
(5 minutes)

After students arrive, invite them to add words to the board or newsprint where you are creating a list of "encouraging words" (phrases or comments that compliment or comfort people). Then ask, Which of these do you use? Which do you receive? How do you feel afterwards? What is more common: to build up or put down?

PROFILE OF AN ENCOURAGER
(15 minutes)

Today's lesson looks at a man named Joseph (Barnabas). His name means "Son of Encouragement." Notice how he encouraged others. Ask a student to read Acts 4:32–37. Use the student page to create a profile of the Son of Encouragement. Look back at Acts 1–4. Then lead a discussion using the following questions:

When did the events of the reading take place? (From after Jesus' resurrection until shortly after Pentecost.) Describe what it was like to be part of this Early Church. (People were one in heart and mind; they loved God and each other; people shared the message of Jesus and shared their possessions.)

How did these Christians care for the needy? (They sold their possessions and distributed the profits.) The "great power" and "much grace" of God (verse 33) also touched Joseph.

ENCOURAGER IN ACTION
(15 Minutes)

Joseph became known as Barnabas, Son of Encouragement. His faith was produced by the Holy Spirit—the Encourager/Comforter that Jesus promised to send (see John 16:7–11). Barnabas lived up to his name not just through his financial gift recorded in Acts 4, but in other ways as well.

Read Acts 11:19–30 and then discuss the questions on the student page.

Barnabas was sent to encourage other believers. When he arrived in Antioch, he "saw the evidence of the grace of God" (verse 23). He encouraged these believers to remain faithful to Jesus. He encouraged Paul not only by introducing him to the Jerusalem Church some years before (Acts 9:26–27), but also by inviting him to assist him in the ministry of the Antioch Church. Barnabas encouraged these Christians to encourage those in need at Jerusalem by sending money for food. Clearly, by the power of the Holy Spirit, Barnabas was an "energized encourager," responding in faith and in action!

ENCOURAGEMENT AMONG US (15 minutes)

As a group, read and discuss the passages on the student page. Students should see that God is the believer's source of encouragement and comfort through the Holy Spirit who works through God's Word and the Sacraments.

Discuss how God leads us to encourage faith in others. Who energizes you to encourage others? What encouragement has God's Word given you today? What could our youth group do to serve God as "energized encouragers"?

CLOSING (5 minutes)

Read together Psalm 121, one of the great psalms of encouragement. Or pray the collect for the minor festival of St. Barnabas celebrated on June 11 (*LW*, p. 97).

Energized Encouragers!

PROFILE OF AN ENCOURAGER
Read **Acts 4:32–37**. Who was this Joseph? Place the items from the list under one of the headings.

One of the twelve apostles
Nicknamed Joseph
Converted after Pentecost
A Gentile
A tax collector
From Galilee
From Cyprus
A Jew
Nicknamed Barnabas

HE WAS

HE WAS NOT

ENCOURAGER IN ACTION
Read **Acts 11:19–30**.

Why was Barnabas sent to Antioch?

Describe the situation he found when he arrived there.

How did he encourage these believers?

Who else was encouraged in **Acts 9:26–27**?

How did Barnabas help the Antioch Christians encourage other believers?

Who energized Barnabas to encourage others?

ENCOURAGEMENT AMONG US
The encouraging words we often hear are just social niceties or politeness. What insight do these encouraging words from the Word of God provide about real encouragement?

Acts 9:31

Romans 15:4–7

2 Corinthians 1:3–7

2 Thessalonians 2:16–17

Journey of Faith © 2007 Concordia Publishing House. Reproduced by permission.

STUDENT PAGE 46

47. GOD'S GIFT

Acts 11:19–30

Lesson Focus

God is at work in the world, choosing and equipping people to share His gift of the Gospel. Young people are blessed to receive, and to be channels for, God's gift of grace.

ONLY 217 MORE SHOPPING DAYS 'TIL CHRISTMAS (15 minutes)

Distribute copies of the student page. Discuss Christmas gift giving using the activities in this section.

NAMES AND GIFTS (20 minutes)

Have the students read the Bible passages and discuss the questions. (You may wish to do this in small groups, followed by brief reports and review.) Make the following points during discussion:

1. Many names have special meaning. Being named after others creates strong connections between those named and those they are named after. In Antioch, believers were first called "Christians," revealing their connection with Christ and all He had done for them.
2. The most familiar "gifts" on the Ephesians list will be pastors and teachers. They build up the Church through God's Word. To build up the Antioch Christians, the Church in Jerusalem first sent Barnabas. Then Barnabas sought out Saul.
3. As you review the story of Saul/Paul, emphasize how nasty Saul was, how little he deserved God's forgiveness, how amazing his change in character, and especially how far in advance God prepared him as a gift for the people in Antioch. The dates are uncertain, but God was clearly working years in advance.

OPENING AND SHARING OUR GIFTS (15 minutes)

Point out that the Ephesians list of "gifts" refers primarily to those who serve in Word and Sacrament ministries in the Church, but also implies that those volunteers in the Church who teach God's Word are also "gifts" from God. (1) Encourage students to name the pastor(s), other full-time church workers, and volunteer teachers they know in your congregation. (2) Point out that some receive special training for full-time service, while others serve as best they are able with local training. If there is time, you might tell how God prepared you to be a gift to the Church. Bring out that we all need people to nurture our faith, comfort us in grief, inspire us with their own faith, or instruct us in the way of God's heart. (3) Answers will vary. Encourage students to seriously consider how God might be calling them to serve Him, perhaps even in full-time church work. (4) Have fun choosing new names like "Wide-smiling-usher" or "One-who-tells-God-stories-to-toddlers-in-the-grass." Think of a name for yourself as an example.

CLOSING (5 minutes)

Pray the following prayer, pausing at the blank to let students speak names of their choice. (You could also include the names of everyone in your class.)

"Lord Jesus, thank You for sending people to be Your gifts to us. Thank You for (volunteered names). Continue to encourage and nurture us with Your gifts of grace and prepare us to be Your gifts to others, reflecting Your love. Amen."

LESSON EXTENDER

✝ Talk extensively about church work careers. Seek information from your church's regional or national headquarters, or invite a church work professional to talk about his or her work with the class.

✝ Write a thank-you note to your pastor, director of Christian education, or teacher. Or write a thank-you prayer for that person and send him or her a copy.

God's Gift

ONLY 217 MORE SHOPPING DAYS 'TIL CHRISTMAS

Write down the names of people you usually buy Christmas gifts for and, by each name, come up with a couple of gift ideas.

Which statement best describes your gift-planning strategy?

___ I start planning for the next Christmas the day after the last one.

___ I wait until mid-summer and then start thinking and buying.

___ I don't really think about it until Thanksgiving.

___ I make a careful list of names and ideas and try to stick to the list.

___ Three words: "Catalogs! Catalogs! Catalogs!"

___ I just hit the stores and buy what strikes me at the moment.

___ I just hit the stores and hope to find something just to get it all over with.

___ Yeow! Christmas Eve already? I gotta hit the mall!

___ I send someone out to hit the stores for me.

___ Gifts?? Bah! Humbug!

NAMES AND GIFTS

1. Read **Acts 11:19–30**—here the Antioch believers are given a name. What name were they given? What does that name imply about them? What does that name imply about you?

2. The new believers in Antioch needed to be built up in spiritual strength. Read **Ephesians 4:7–8, 11–12**. According to Paul, what gifts does God provide His Church to build it up? Through whom does God provide for the Antioch Christians' needs?

3. Read **Galatians 1:13; 2:1;** and **Acts 9:1–20**. What was Saul's purpose in life before his encounter with Jesus? Why did that purpose change?

OPENING AND SHARING OUR GIFTS

1. What sort of "gifts" (in the Ephesians 4 sense) has God given your church? (Write down their *names*.)

2. How did they become gifts God could bring to your church? How have they been gifts to you or people you know?

3. The Antioch Christians received God's gift of the Gospel. They also shared their blessings with others **(Acts 11:28–30)**. Saul received God's gift and shared it throughout Asia Minor. What gifts have you received from God? (Check the "inventories" in **Galatians 5:22–23** or **Romans 12:3–8**.)

4. Saul is better known by his other name, Paul. In many traditions, including some Native American ones, people pick names at some point in life that have particular meaning to them. If you picked a new name that would describe how you are a gift to the Church, what would that name be?

Journey of Faith © 2007 Concordia Publishing House. Reproduced by permission.

48. God, a Guy Named Timothy, and Me

Acts 16:1–5; 2 Timothy 1:5–7; 3:14–16

Lesson Focus

Believers are called to service in God's kingdom, regardless of age.

LAST WILL AND TESTAMENT (15 minutes)

A note to the leader: Before beginning this activity, be sensitive to students who may have recently lost a loved one or who may have contemplated ending their own lives. As an alternative in this situation, draft a "will" from the whole group.

Have students draw up a draft of their own will. What items/objects, wisdom/advice would they pass on to the next class or youth group? Have students choose one thing from their will to share with the group.

A CLOSER LOOK AT TIMOTHY AND A CLOSER LOOK AT ME (30 minutes)

Most likely, 2 Timothy is the last Letter Paul wrote before his death. In it, Paul entrusts the Gospel to his "son in the faith," Timothy. Read Acts 16:1–5; 2 Timothy 1:5–7; and 3:14–16. Timothy was in his teens when he joined Paul's missionary crew (see *Concordia Self-Study Bible* note on Acts 16:1). What risks was Timothy facing by joining the group? (Persecution, opposition) On a scale of 1 to 10, with 10 being the most, how serious is Timothy's commitment to his decision to join Paul's ministry? Be prepared to explain your answer. (Answers will vary; it should be a high number, considering his reputation and his circumcision.) In what ways have you personally experienced or heard about God working through mission trips? Have you ever considered serving God as a missionary or church worker? What problems might you encounter as a teenager serving in the Church? What blessings? What ways can you serve God in your congregation even now?

Timothy came from a spiritually "split" home: his mom and grandmother were believers, while his father most likely was not. Does this situation make it easier or harder to be a Christian? Why? Timothy's faith is called "sincere" in 2 Timothy 1:5. What does this tell us about the nature of faith? (It comes from God; He works in and through our circumstances.) How has God used your family circumstances to develop your faith? Who are the spiritual mentors in your life that God has worked through?

Timothy lacked self-assurance (2 Timothy 1:7; 1 Corinthians 16:10–11; 1 Timothy 4:12), but he also had been given a spiritual gift from God to develop and "fan into flame." How might God have used both Timothy's weakness and his spiritual gift to further the Gospel? (Answers will vary.) What does this tell us about God? (When we are weak, He is strong.) Where is your weakness? You have also been given gifts and talents to "fan into flame." What are some ways you can develop your gifts and talents? (Answers will vary.)

CLOSING (5 minutes)

"Gracious God, we know that You are our God and we are Your people. Forgive us for trying to live like we are not Yours. We know You have great plans for us to serve You. We pray that by Your power You would overcome our fears and work in us. May we serve You by serving those around us every day. We pray in Jesus' name. Amen."

LESSON EXTENDER

✝ Read together or sing the words of "Hark, the Voice of Jesus Calling" (*LSB* 827; *LW* 318).

God, a Guy Named Timothy, and Me

LAST WILL AND TESTAMENT
Draft your youth group will. What items/objects, wisdom/advice would you pass on to the next class or youth group?

....
....
....
....
....

A CLOSER LOOK AT TIMOTHY AND A CLOSER LOOK AT ME

Most likely, 2 Timothy is the last Letter Paul wrote before his death. In it, Paul entrusts the Gospel to his "son in the faith," Timothy. Read **Acts 16:1–5**; **2 Timothy 1:5–7**; and **3:14–16**.

Timothy was in his teens when he joined Paul's missionary crew. What risks was Timothy facing by joining the group?

....

On a scale of 1 to 10, with 10 being the most, how serious is Timothy's commitment to his decision to join Paul's ministry? Be prepared to explain your answer.

....

In what ways have you personally experienced or heard about God working through mission trips?

....

What missions or ministries are you drawn to?

....

What problems might you encounter as a teenager serving in a mission or ministry? What blessings?

....

Timothy came from a spiritually "split" home: his mom and grandmother were believers, while his father most likely was not. Does this situation make it easier or harder to be a Christian? Why?

....

Timothy's faith is called "sincere" in **2 Timothy 1:5**. What does this tell us about the nature of faith?

....

How has God used your family circumstances to develop your faith?

....

Who are the spiritual mentors in your life that God has worked through?

....

Timothy lacked self-assurance **(2 Timothy 1:7; 1 Corinthians 16:10–11; 1 Timothy 4:12)**, but he also had been given a spiritual gift from God to develop and "fan into flame." How might God have used both Timothy's weakness and his spiritual gift to further the Gospel?

....

What does this tell us about God?

....

Where is your weakness?

....

You have also been given gifts and talents to "fan into flame." What are some ways you can develop your gifts and talents?

....

Journey of Faith © 2007 Concordia Publishing House. Reproduced by permission.

49. This Way or That Way?

Acts 16:6–15
Lesson Focus
God directs our path to fulfill His purposes.

THIS WAY OR THAT WAY? (10 minutes)

In this activity, students have two options in the form of a question. They need to choose the one they prefer and be prepared to explain their choice. It may be helpful to write each question on the board or newsprint. After students have had a chance to think about each question, ask them to move "this way" (against one wall) if they picked the first option or "that way" (the opposing wall) if they picked the second. Let individuals in each group explain their choices. For a less active opening, ask students to respond to the choice pairs without moving.

Would you rather . . .

see God or hear His voice?

not know what you *should* do or know what you are *not* supposed to do?

fail before you succeed or never fail yet never succeed?

WHICH WAY? (15 minutes)

Distribute copies of the student page. Work as a whole group to discuss the first question. Student answers will vary depending on their level of Bible knowledge. Be prepared to provide examples of your own.

Read aloud Acts 16:6–15. In breakout groups, have students consider the remaining questions in this section of the student page; then have groups share their thoughts with the class. The text doesn't say how Paul and his crew were directed away from traveling to Asia and Bithynia. How has God acted throughout Scripture to direct His people? (People—leaders, judges, prophets; Political/social circumstances—the exodus, Roman census, captivity; Divine revelation—signs, visions, spoke directly, Bible; Weather—Jonah, Paul) What may have been some typical human reactions Paul and his crew may have had to their apparent "setbacks"? (Answers will vary.) What were the reactions of Lydia (verses 13–15) and later the Philippian jailer (verse 34) after their Baptism? (Gracious hospitality and joy.) What was God's plan in all of this? (He wants us to be faithful; He will bless our work and bring about the success He desires.)

FOLLOWING GOD'S WAY! (20 minutes)

Have students work individually to consider the questions in this section. Allow time for individuals to share their answers about how God has directed them in the past. When we fail to follow God's direction, we often feel frustrated and alone. The words of Proverbs 3:5–6 remind the believer how much God cares about us and wants to lead us by the power of His Spirit. Encourage students to share areas where they feel the Spirit is leading them in the future.

CLOSING (5 minutes)

Pray, "Powerful Father, You know the past, present, and future. You know our steps before we take them. Show us the path to follow every day. We know that walking by Your Spirit is the only way to live. Lead us to follow You. In Jesus' name. Amen." Sing or read together the words to "'Come, Follow Me,' the Savior Spake" (*LSB* 688; *LW* 379).

LESSON EXTENDER

✝ Encourage students to memorize Proverbs 3:5–6.

This Way or That Way?

WHICH WAY?
How has God acted throughout Scripture to direct His people?

People—

....

....

Political/social circumstances—

....

....

Divine revelation—

....

....

Weather—

....

....

Other—

....

....

Read **Acts 16:6–15**.

What may have been some typical human reactions Paul and his crew may have had to their apparent "setbacks"?

....

What were the reactions of Lydia **(verses 13–15)** and later the Philippian jailer **(verse 34)** after their Baptism?

....

....

What was God's plan in all of this?

....

....

FOLLOWING GOD'S WAY!
How has God directed you in the past concerning

friends?

....

career?

....

spiritual growth?

....

dating?

....

What was the result of following or not following God's direction?

....

Considering **Proverbs 3:5–6**, how can painful obstacles, defeats, refusals, or disappointments be reassuring to a Christian?

How might God be directing you in these areas now?

....

....

Friends

....

Spiritual growth

....

Career

....

Dating

....

Journey of Faith © 2007 Concordia Publishing House. Reproduced by permission.

50. Fearless Faith

Acts 16:16–40

Lesson Focus

It can be risky for young people to share their faith in Christ, let alone defend it. This lesson reminds us that God promises to strengthen our faith and support us as we have opportunities to share His message and love with others.

HAVE YOU EVER? (5 minutes)

Use the checklist on the student page to discuss students' attempts to share their faith. Do students have a lack of opportunities to share their faith? Or do they avoid opportunities that arise? Explore with students what fears hinder them from sharing their faith.

REAL-LIFE FAITH CHALLENGES (15 minutes)

Discuss with students the real-life examples described. If possible, be prepared to share recent examples of young Christians who have met opposition to their faith.

PAUL'S STRUGGLES (15 minutes)

Have students work alone or with partners to complete this section. Have pairs share their insights with the whole group. Paul was trying to go to the place of prayer (verse 16). Despite Paul's struggles, God used Paul to share Jesus and bring the jailer and his entire household into the family of God.

GOD'S PROMISES (15 minutes)

Romans 8 reminds us that we can have confidence in God because of all He has done and continues to do in our lives in spite of our trials. Have students work in pairs to explore the selected verses of Romans 8 found on the student page. Have partners share the promises they find in the Word.

Conclude this section by saying, "When it comes to sharing or defending our faith, it would be easy to be overwhelmed with fear. But God doesn't want us to face struggles on our own. He invites us to depend on Him. He promises to help us and to always be with us."

NO FEAR (5 minutes)

Provide index cards on which students can write the Bible verse of their choice. Encourage students to use the note cards in the next week to help them memorize the verse.

CLOSING (5 minutes)

Close with silent prayer. Suggest that students confess their fears to God. Remind them of the forgiveness that is theirs through Jesus Christ.

LESSON EXTENDER

Plan an activity outside of class (such as calling on church visitors, canvassing a neighborhood, or visiting a hospital or homeless shelter) to challenge teens beyond their comfort zones as well as to offer opportunities to share Jesus.

Fearless Faith

HAVE YOU EVER?

Have you ever . . .

worn a Christian T-shirt or Christian jewelry?	Yes	No
visited a hospital or nursing home?	Yes	No
talked about Jesus with a stranger?	Yes	No
talked about Jesus with a friend?	Yes	No
gone on a mission trip?	Yes	No
volunteered at a homeless shelter?	Yes	No
prayed at school?	Yes	No

REAL-LIFE FAITH CHALLENGES

A sophomore is belittled for wearing a T-shirt that shows Jesus bleeding on the cross.

A 15-year-old girl receives a low grade after refusing to write an essay on the topic "I'd sell my soul to the devil in order to . . ."

Two varsity baseball players are benched for failing to attend a practice on Good Friday.

A high school valedictorian is warned to remove any references to faith in Jesus Christ from the graduation day speech.

Students are shot, some fatally, while meeting in a school prayer group.

PAUL'S STRUGGLES

In the New Testament, Paul faced many struggles as he tried to share the message of Jesus Christ. Read **Acts 16:16–34**.

What was Paul trying to do?

What trials or struggles did he face?

What was the outcome?

GOD'S PROMISES

Nowhere in Scripture does God promise us trouble-free lives. In **Romans 8**, what does He promise instead?

Verses 1–17

Verse 28

Verse 31

Verses 37–39

NO FEAR

Choose one of the verses from Romans (or any other Bible verse) as your "fearless faith" reminder when you are challenged to share Jesus.

Journey of Faith © 2007 Concordia Publishing House. Reproduced by permission.

51. IS IGNORANCE BLISS?

Acts 17:1–34

Lesson Focus

God desires all to be saved. He uses us, His children, as His instruments to witness to those who do not yet know Him as Lord.

OPENING (10 minutes)

Ask, "You may have heard the saying 'ignorance is bliss.' Where would this phrase apply? What are some occasions where this is *not* true?" Our society continues to become more and more postmodern—where right and wrong are subjective and not absolute. While sometimes a person may prefer to be blissfully ignorant of the spinach stuck between his or her teeth, choosing to be blissfully ignorant of the almighty God has much different consequences.

PAUL'S WITNESS IN ATHENS (15 minutes)

Distribute copies of the student page. Have students work with partners to read the Scripture verses and answer the questions from this section. Review with the whole group. In Athens, Paul was witnessing among superstitious polytheists. In contrast, in both Thessalonica and Berea he spoke to Jews and God-fearing Gentiles who knew the Creator God. The Athenians were like many people in our culture who do not know the almighty Creator.

FIRST COMMANDMENT CLASH (15 minutes)

It is common in our day to hear the opinion "It really doesn't matter *what* you believe, as long as you are sincere." In postmodern thought it is wrong to "impose" one's beliefs onto another.

The Athenians were trying to cover all the bases by building an altar to honor an "unknown god." Paul knew the First Commandment, "You shall have no other gods." This commandment helps to motivate Christian witness—when God is not being worshiped, the First Commandment is broken.

Have students role-play. Divide into two sides. One side is to advocate Paul's witness about the true God in the culture that welcomed any (and all) religious teachings. The other side is to defend that the Athenians' effort should be enough to satisfy God.

The First Commandment leaves no room for misunderstanding. It is a clear statement of absolutes. Use this role play to help the students in their witness. While we don't see altars to unknown gods in twenty-first-century America, many Americans are just as ignorant of the almighty Creator God as were the Athenians.

MOVING AHEAD (10 minutes)

Have students work individually on this section. God gives us daily opportunities to testify that He alone is God. Paul saw the altar to the unknown god as an opportunity to tell the Athenians about the true God. Through His Spirit and the Word, God provides us the resources and power to witness about Jesus Christ, our Savior.

Spend time in prayer asking for God's guidance and strength to see the opportunities He gives each of us to witness for Him.

LESSON EXTENDER

✝ Read the First Commandment in *Luther's Small Catechism with Explanation* and accompanying questions and Bible passages to aid the students in their witnessing.

IS IGNORANCE BLISS?

PAUL'S WITNESS IN ATHENS

Read Paul's witness to the Athenians in **Acts 17:16–34**. The Athenians worshiped a lot of "gods," so many gods that they realized that there was probably an "unknown god" they should revere.

How is Paul's witness in Athens different than when he talked in Thessalonica and Berea (see **Acts 17:1–4, 10–12**)?

....

....

....

What was the reaction of the Athenians?

....

....

MOVING AHEAD

What opportunities do you have among your family, friends, co-workers, and neighbors to help dissolve their ignorance about Jesus Christ?

....

....

....

Pray for the Holy Spirit to open their hearts to the truth, and pray for faithfulness in responding to upcoming opportunities to witness.

STUDENT PAGE 51

Journey of Faith © 2007 Concordia Publishing House. Reproduced by permission.

52. GOD IS IN CONTROL

Acts 27–28

Lesson Focus

Through Paul's stormy journey to Rome, we find hope that God prevails even in the storms of life.

WHAT'S YOUR WEATHER METER? (5 minutes)

Distribute copies of the student page. Allow time for youth to choose a weather report. Invite youth to share the reason for their choice.

A STORMY JOURNEY (15 minutes)

God had told Paul that he would go to Rome. Paul may have expected the journey to be without conflict.

Divide students into five groups. Assign each group one of the five passages from the student page. Have students determine the obstacles to the journey, Paul's response, and evidence of God's presence and purpose (His grace within the obstacle). Have groups discuss their answers with the whole class.

Acts 27:1–12: Winds against them; slow travel; too late in the season for ship travel. Paul warns men of upcoming danger. God is laying the foundation for a great rescue at sea where Paul could witness about God's power and love.

Acts 27:13–15; 20–26: Hurricane winds blow the ship off course; men are afraid and hopeless. Paul urges men to be courageous; says God has revealed that lives will not be lost. God sends an angel to Paul; promises to save all aboard.

Acts 27:27–44: Sailors try to escape ship; weakness from lack of food; ship runs aground on sandbar and begins to break up; soldiers want to kill prisoners. Paul guides sailors; urges men to eat; models courage and hope; reminds them they will be safe. God gives Paul wisdom to know what men are scheming to do; keeps Paul calm and able to direct and encourage the men; guides the centurion to protect Paul from the soldiers.

Acts 28:1–11: Cold, rainy weather; snake bites Paul; on island for three months. Paul shows no fear; works alongside others; heals father of host, which enables him to witness during the time there. God allowed many to be saved and healed; Paul had no ill effect from snake bite; people opened their homes to the men (all 276 of them!) for three months.

Acts 28:16–20, 24: Paul under house arrest, no charge given. Paul uses the opportunity to preach the Gospel. God used Paul to convince some people of the truth of the Gospel.

RAYS OF HOPE (5 minutes)

Choose two students to read aloud **Acts 23:11** and **Acts 28:30–31**. Discuss questions on the student page together. God allowed Paul to give witness about Jesus in Rome.

GOD'S FORECAST (10 minutes)

Pair students to work together on the activity from the student page. Have each pair share what they discussed.

PREVAILING THROUGH THE STORMS OF LIFE (10 minutes)

Allow a full five minutes for individual quiet meditation upon the questions on the student page. Invite youth to share their thoughts.

CLOSING (5 minutes)

Invite each student to pray aloud a few words of praise for a way that God's plan has unfolded in his or her or someone else's life, or pray that God will take care of a specific situation.

LESSON EXTENDER

✝ Use pictures or words cut from magazines to create a collage showing possible obstacles we face in living a Christlike life.

✝ Write a modern-day paraphrase of the story.

GOD IS IN CONTROL

WHAT'S YOUR WEATHER METER?
In terms of a weather report, how would you describe your life right now? (Be prepared to share your choice.)

_____ Sunny and warm   _____ Stormy
_____ Hot and humid   _____ Scattered showers
_____ Cloudy, but fair   _____ Hurricane warning!

A STORMY JOURNEY

Acts Passage	What are the storms Paul faced?	What was Paul's response?	How do you see God's purpose prevail?
Acts 27:1–12			
Acts 27:13–15, 20–26			
Acts 27:27–44			
Acts 28:1–11			
Acts 28:16–20, 24			

RAYS OF HOPE
Compare **Acts 23:11** and **Acts 28:30–31**. Was God's purpose for sending Paul to Rome accomplished? Why or why not?

GOD'S FORECAST
Look up **Jeremiah 29:11** and **Proverbs 19:21**. Jot down the main ideas in each. How do these verses relate to our discussion? What do these promises of God mean for your life?

PREVAILING THROUGH THE STORMS OF LIFE
What is the greatest storm in your life right now? How can Paul's example help you?

How can knowing that God has a plan for you and that His purposes will prevail help you as you consider this storm?

STUDENT PAGE 52

Journey of Faith © 2007 Concordia Publishing House. Reproduced by permission.